Battle Colors

BATTLE COLORS

Insignia And Aircraft Markings Of
The Eighth Air Force In World War II

Volume I/ (VIII) Bomber Command

Robert A. Watkins

Schiffer Military History
Atglen, PA

To My Wife Karen...
Without whose encouragement and assistance this work
would be little more than a random mass of many years'
worth of personal notes and miscellaneous memorabilia

Book Design & Illustrations by Robert A. Watkins.

Copyright © 2004 by Robert A. Watkins.
Library of Congress Control Number: 2003116219

Printed in China.
ISBN: 0-7643-1987-6

For the largest selection of fine reference books on this and related subjects, please visit our website - **www.schifferbooks.com** - or call for a free catalog.

We are interested in hearing from authors with book ideas on related topics.

Published by Schiffer Publishing Ltd.
4880 Lower Valley Road
Atglen, PA 19310
Phone: (610) 593-1777
FAX: (610) 593-2002
E-mail: Info@schifferbooks.com.
Visit our web site at: www.schifferbooks.com
Please write for a free catalog.
This book may be purchased from the publisher.
Please include $3.95 postage.
Try your bookstore first.

In Europe, Schiffer books are distributed by:
Bushwood Books
6 Marksbury Avenue
Kew Gardens
Surrey TW9 4JF
England
Phone: 44 (0) 20 8392-8585
FAX: 44 (0) 20 8392-9876
E-mail: info@bushwoodbooks.co.uk.
Free postage in the UK. Europe: air mail at cost.
Try your bookstore first.

Contents

INTRODUCTION

It is not the intention of this work to attempt to answer every question concerning the Eighth Air Force during World War Two. It is safe to say that the information contained within the confines of these pages is neither unique nor previously unpublished. What is novel about this work is the manner in which the selected information has been organized and presented to the reader. The purpose of this book is to fill what was perceived as a void that previously existed in available material dealing with a specific aspect of the U.S. Eighth Air Force. What I hope I have provided the reader with is an easy to use reference tool that relies primarily upon visual images rather than text to clarify the organizational structure of the greatest war time air armada ever assembled.

Visual images provided the means by which this massive organization was able to coordinate its efforts in the air. It was thus concluded that an emphasis on visuals would be the logical means with which to tell this particuliar aspect of the Eighth AF story. Hopefully, this effort will be of use to anyone with an interest in the subject of the Eighth, whether that interest be casual or scholastic in nature.

The focus of this work is confined to the principle combat bombardment groups whose duties entailed overt tactical and strategic operations against Hitler's 'Festung Europa'. Omitted in this study are any number of 'special operations' Heavy Bomber units whose duties fell outside the scope of normal combat operations. Also omitted are the legions of support units assigned to each Army Air Force group. Although the contribution these units made in the successful prosecution of the war against Germany was indispensable, they never the less fall outside the main focus of this volume.

The first thing one becomes aware of in the study of this subject is the contrast between the early war A A F paint schemes and identification methods as opposed to those applied as the war progressed. In 1942, AAF bombers displayed little more than the national insignia on fuselage and wing surface areas and the individual aircraft identification number stenciled to either side of the vertical stabilizer. This altogether austere array of markings were applied over fully painted aircraft which would typically vary in configuration from two-color to three-color camoflague.

United States Army Air Force/Material Command, Wright Field, Ohio issued a directive in 1940 which specified colors to be used by all AAF aircraft;

[I.] Airframe and Wing Components:
  [a.] Olive Drab, Dark, No.41
  [b.] Green, Medium, No.42
  [c.] Gray, Neutral, No.43

[II] National Insignia:
  [a.] Red, Insignia, No.45
  [b.] White, Insignia, No.46
  [c.] Blue, Insignia, No.47

[III] Aircraft Identification:
  [a.] Gray, Neutral, No. 43
  [b.] Black, No.44
  [c.] White, Insignia, No.46
  [d.] Yellow, Identification, No.48

These specifications remained, for the most part, unchanged until December 1943. At this time Material Command ordered that the use of camouflage paint on all AAF aircraft be discontinued and further directed the removal of same from aircraft then deployed in all theatres of operation.

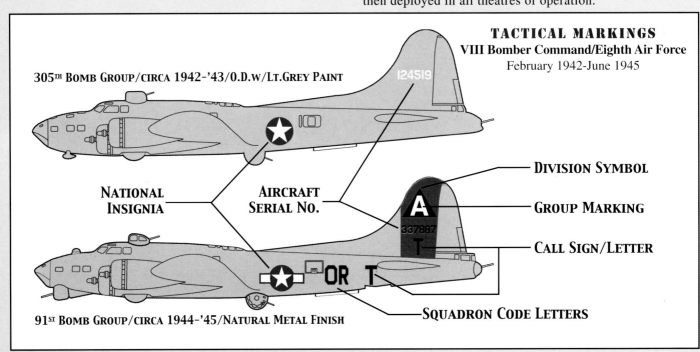

TACTICAL MARKINGS
VIII Bomber Command/Eighth Air Force
February 1942-June 1945

305ᵗʰ Bomb Group/circa 1942-'43/O.D.w/Lt.Grey Paint

124519

NATIONAL INSIGNIA

AIRCRAFT SERIAL No.

DIVISION SYMBOL

GROUP MARKING

CALL SIGN/LETTER

SQUADRON CODE LETTERS

91ˢᵗ Bomb Group/circa 1944-'45/Natural Metal Finish

337887

The official explanation for this decision stated certain logistical advantages. In the case of AAF Bombers, eliminating full camouflage paint schemes reduced overall aircraft weight by an estimated 70-80 pounds resulting in extended range and increased air speeds. Savings in materials as well as man-hours were additional benefits connected with the elimination of camouflaging. Although these benefits were very real, they were not the sole motivation behind this decision. The simple fact was that this order reflected the growing dominance of Allied air power in the skies over Europe and the Pacific. This fact coupled with the greatly diminished threat of bombardment of their own airfields by the Luftwaffe effectively eliminated the need for the Eighth AF to continue camouflaging its' aircraft.

In direct contrast to this diminishing need for aircraft paint was the ever increasing need for improved unit and individual aircraft identification. The days of single group raids were pretty much a thing of the past as far as Eighth AF operations were concerned.

By mid 1944 the skies over Europe could, at any given time, be filled with upwards to a thousand heavy bombers, all intent on converging upon a single target in one massive coordinated effort. Add to the complexity of such an effort the hundreds of fighter escorts that were required to rendezvous with their assigned bomb groups in order to fly protective top cover both to and from the target area and one can easily grasp the critical need for visual airborne identification.

Yet to be discussed is the most basic of all military aircraft identification, the national insignia. The USAAF National insignia underwent numerous official and semiofficial changes within a two year period, but in one form or another, these symbols were displayed on all AAF aircraft throughout the war.

Although U.S. National insignia can be helpful in establishing the time period of a particular Eighth AF photo, it is important for the researcher not to jump to any conclusions based upon this evidence alone. Due to shortages in manpower and/or materials, changes in aircraft marking policy were often not immediately acted upon at a group level. During World War One the United States Army Air Service began operations with a national insignia device consisting of a small red circle centered on a white star centered on a blue disk. At the urging of than Col. William 'Billy' Mitchell this symbol was changed to a roundel device on January 18, 1918. This design was very similar in appearance to those national emblems applied to both French and British warplanes and the similarity was thought to be an advantage at that time.

Following WWI the Army unofficially reverted to the original blue disc and white star design in 1919. In 1920 the Army Reorganization Act designated the Air Service as a combat arm of the U.S. Army. At this time the disk and star configuration was officially adopted and would remain in continued use for the next twenty years.

The outbreak of World War Two created an immediate need for a change in U.S. aircraft identification. The first modification was the elimination of the red disk from the center of the white star. It was discovered early on that this tended to draw friendly fire from antiaircraft gunners who mistook the red disk for the Hinomaru or 'meatball', the national insignia displayed on all Japanese military aircraft. Also eliminated was the red, white and blue vertical and horizontal stripes previously found on the tail sections of U.S. Army and Navy warplanes. It was further decided to cease the application of the national insignia from the lower left and upper right wing surfaces as this tended to present enemy gunners and pilots with what is known as a 'balanced aiming point'.

Reviewing the various changes and modifications to the national insignia in 1942 more or less graphically illustrates the turmoil and transition, the state of utter confusion the United States underwent in the earliest phases of World War Two. The decision to modify the national insignia was by no means arbitrary and in fact involved considerable research and extensive field testing by both the Army and Navy in order to properly evaluate the numerous proposed design changes.

The national insignia adopted in September, 1943 would remain in effect, unchanged, for the wars duration.

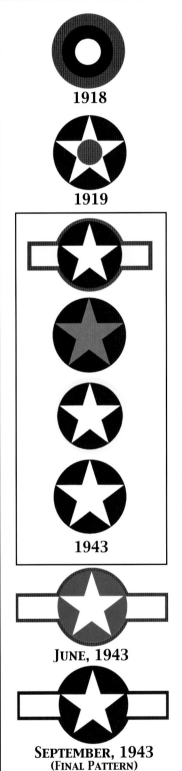

1918

1919

1943

JUNE, 1943

SEPTEMBER, 1943
(FINAL PATTERN)

It should be pointed out that the illustrations contained within this text are approximations of their full size counterparts upon which they were based. This fact may be of particular significance to those readers who's interest lies within the realm of scale modeling. While every care was taken to keep all elements contained within each rendering as accurate as possible, they are when all is said and done, illustrations, not engineering drawings. That said it would behove anyone bent upon absolute accuracy to contact the respective government agencies and obtain, if available, the necessary technical drawings and/or specification sheets relating to their particular area of interest. On the other hand it should be noted that even though the Army Air Corps had very specific guidelines when it came to the size, shape and color of national emblems and tactical markings in relationship to the application of same to its' aircraft, these rules were often only loosely adhered to. This was especially true in the early phases of World War II and most especially true of first line combat units and the direct result in large part to the shortage of both manpower and materials. A close evaluation of period photographs will often reveal subtle to blatant variations when it came to sizes, configurations and placement of aircraft markings from one group to another, one squadron to another. It is these very same variations, however, that makes the study of this subject so fascinating. The deeper one delves into this area the more interesting it tends to become.

The photo below appears to be the right rear fuselage of a battle damaged B-17F and bears testament to some of the multiformity which ensued in the early stages of the Eighth Air Forces' deployment in England during WWII. The outer ring of the national insignia is rendered in Insignia Yellow , the inner disk a medium blue and the star a light gray. This configuration fits somewhere in between several sanctioned insignia versions that appeared on U.S. aircraft between 1942 and June, 1943. Even after this date irregularities can be noted in war time photographs that continued throughout the war. The conclusion to be drawn from all this is simply that only those individuals wishing to produce a scale model of a pristine, fresh-from-the-factory bomber will have to worry to much about religious adherence to Army Air Corps regulations.

•Using This Book•

There should be little problem in this area for anyone with even a casual familiarity with the USAAF in WWII. This work provides the user with a 'visual index' in addition to the text indexing method traditionally found in the back of most reference sources. Those readers who have a visual that they want to identify can simply skip ahead to pages 12 thorough 15. Contained therein are graphic representations of the mid-to-late war tail markings for all B-17 and B-24 Bomb Groups assigned to the Eighth Air Force between 1942 and 1945. All groups are listed in numerical order in the main body of this text, additionally, you will find a numerical listing of all Bomb Groups of The Eighth in addition to charts of Group listings by Wing/Division assignments.

The organizational chart depicted below is symbolic of the format utilized throughout the main portion of this text. It is fairly self explanatory, but again, for those unfamiliar with the structure of the USAAF during this period, a brief orientation may be helpful.

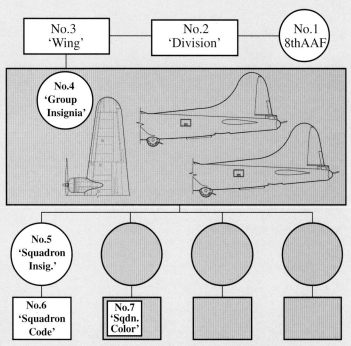

Items one (1) through five (5) illustrate the organizational flow from the overall command down to individual squadron level. Items six (6) and seven (7) are unit markers within the group/squadron level. Once you identify the squadron code of any given aircraft you can easily establish the entire chain of command all the way up the line.

One final note relating to the diagram. A blank space in any of the item slots four (4) thorough seven (7) does not mean that I missed something when doing the final assembly for this book. On any given page an empty space where an insignia, squadron code or color should be simply means that to date that item either never existed or has perhaps fallen into the great historical abyss.

DEFENSIVE BOMBING FORMATIONS

•War Department / Air Corps Field Manual No. FM1-10
'Tactics and Technique of Air Attack'•
•Chapter 2 /'Bombardment Aviation'
•Section VI-'Flight Formations'
•Paragraph 51/'Formation Flying'

'The military airplane is a complete combat unit. Its capabilities are dependent upon its type and the character of its combat equipment. The offensive and defensive powers of even the largest and most powerful individual airplane are relatively limited. Hence the effective utilization of aircraft in warfare frequently requires that they be employed in suitable tactical formations rather than as single units. The organization of aviation forces into suitable tactical units facilitates the simultaneous employment of the aircraft in the accomplishment of an assigned mission'.

•Paragraph 68/'Need for Defensive Formations'•

'Defensive formations are necessary whenever bombardment units are employed during daylight within range of enemy weapons. Such protection is necessary in order to insure the completion of tactical missions in enemy territory and to minimize losses which may result from active opposition'.

**By order of the Secretary of War
G.C. Marshall, Chief of Staff
November 20, 1940**

As this document illustrates, Army Air Corps planners understood the importance of highly organized bombardment formations well before the United States entered the Second World War. This was all the more significant due to the fact that the Army had no first hand heavy bomber combat experience to draw upon. It should be noted here that the Army Air Corps was barely thirty years old at the outbreak of hostilities shortly after Pearl Harbor. The Air Corps aerial combat experience during World War One had been limited to fighter and reconnaissance duties. The concept of large scale, sustained bombardment campaigns was in fact a post World War One development and still very much in an embryonic stage when the United States was thrust into World War Two.

It was a generally held consensus by many within the Air Corps in the early stages of WWII that a well ordered bomber formation was capable of defending itself against virtually any assault by enemy aircraft. The flaw in this thinking became painfully apparent shortly after the Eighth Air Forces initial operations in the summer of 1942. After a great deal of innovative thinking combined with costly trial-and-error experimentation, the Combat Box evolved into what many considered the optimum heavy bomber defensive formation. Once perfected the Combat Box would be employed almost exclusively by the Eighth AF for the duration of the war.

The Combat Box was a complex system of precise airborne configurations designed to optimize the firepower of each aircraft within the collective unit. It required a high degree of training and aircraft handling skills on the part of both pilot and copilot in order to maintain an effective defensive Box formation. Each plane was expected to hold its respective preassigned position within the formation unless ordered to do otherwise. Pilots had to be prepared on a moments notice to maneuver his aircraft within the formation in order to fill gaps created by losses to enemy action or equipment failure. In short, flight crews had to maintain a constant state of readiness from the time they took off until the final touch down at missions end.

The series of three photos below will serve to illustrate all to well the consequences of just one aircraft failing to maintain its proper interval within the heavy bomber 'Box'. This type of mishap was, unfortunately, not an uncommon occurrence among bombers flying in tight defensive formations.

This series of strike photos is a vivid testimony to the devastating potential of a well executed precision daylight bombing raid during World War II.

'THE TARGET'

October 1943; the Focke-Wulf aircraft plant located near Marienburg, Germany. At the time this aerial reconnaissance photo was taken, this particular facility was producing close to 50% of all Fw190 Fighters for the Luftwaffe.

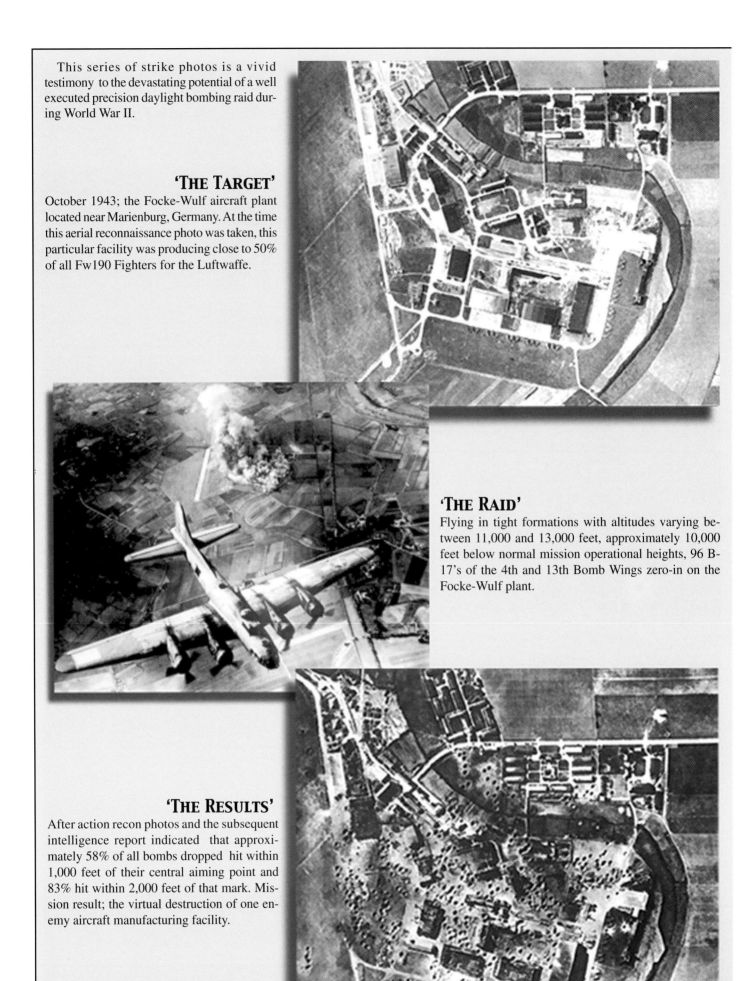

'THE RAID'

Flying in tight formations with altitudes varying between 11,000 and 13,000 feet, approximately 10,000 feet below normal mission operational heights, 96 B-17's of the 4th and 13th Bomb Wings zero-in on the Focke-Wulf plant.

'THE RESULTS'

After action recon photos and the subsequent intelligence report indicated that approximately 58% of all bombs dropped hit within 1,000 feet of their central aiming point and 83% hit within 2,000 feet of that mark. Mission result; the virtual destruction of one enemy aircraft manufacturing facility.

The following diagrams will help illustrate the composition of a typical Combat Box based upon the Squadron Stagger Formation. The first of these show three separate views of a Group level formation. Each colored box represents a squadron, six aircraft to a squadron, three squadrons to a group. Each squadron within the group were staggered in layers in a manner similar to that shown below. As previously mentioned, this was necessary to facilitate both simultaneous release of bomb loads and to maximize the defensive firepower of all aircraft within the formation.

In order to accomplish these complicated aerial maneuvers it was imperative that every ship within the formation be recognizable to all those within the formation. While pilots might be allowed to individualize the nose of his ship with artwork, the remainder of the aircraft was pretty much off limits. Every letter, number, color and pattern had a specific meaning and uniformity of these symbols was imperative to formation flying.

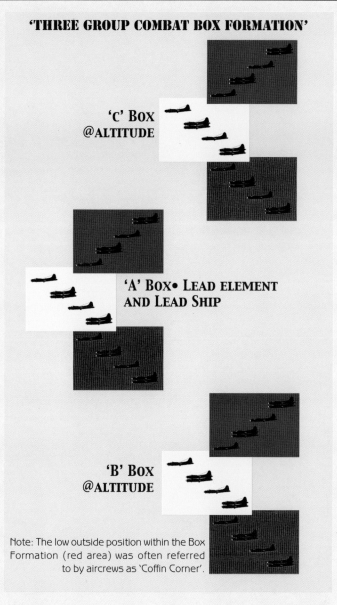

'THREE GROUP COMBAT BOX FORMATION'

'C' BOX
@ALTITUDE

'A' BOX • LEAD ELEMENT AND LEAD SHIP

'B' BOX
@ALTITUDE

Note: The low outside position within the Box Formation (red area) was often referred to by aircrews as 'Coffin Corner'.

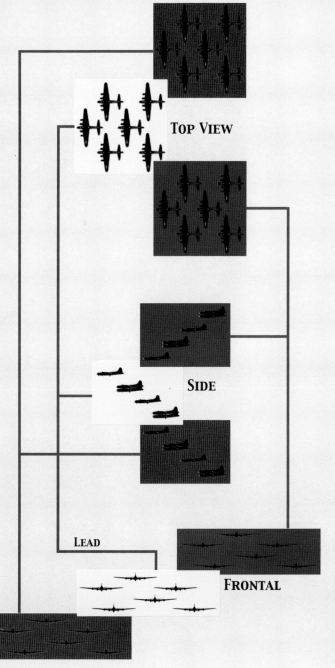

TOP VIEW

SIDE

LEAD

FRONTAL

The photo below illustrates far better than words the narrow margin for error involved in formation flying. It is also an excellent example of unit identification markings.

By simply referencing the Group Symbol Index and turning to the appropriate page, one can quickly determine that this B-17, Serial No.48393 (no nickname), call letter 'Y' was assigned to the 709th Bombardment Squadron/447th Bombardment Group.

While the subject of AAF Defensive Bombardment Formations during World War II may at first seem somewhat beyond the overall scope of this texts primary theme, it was never-the-less considered important that it be included.

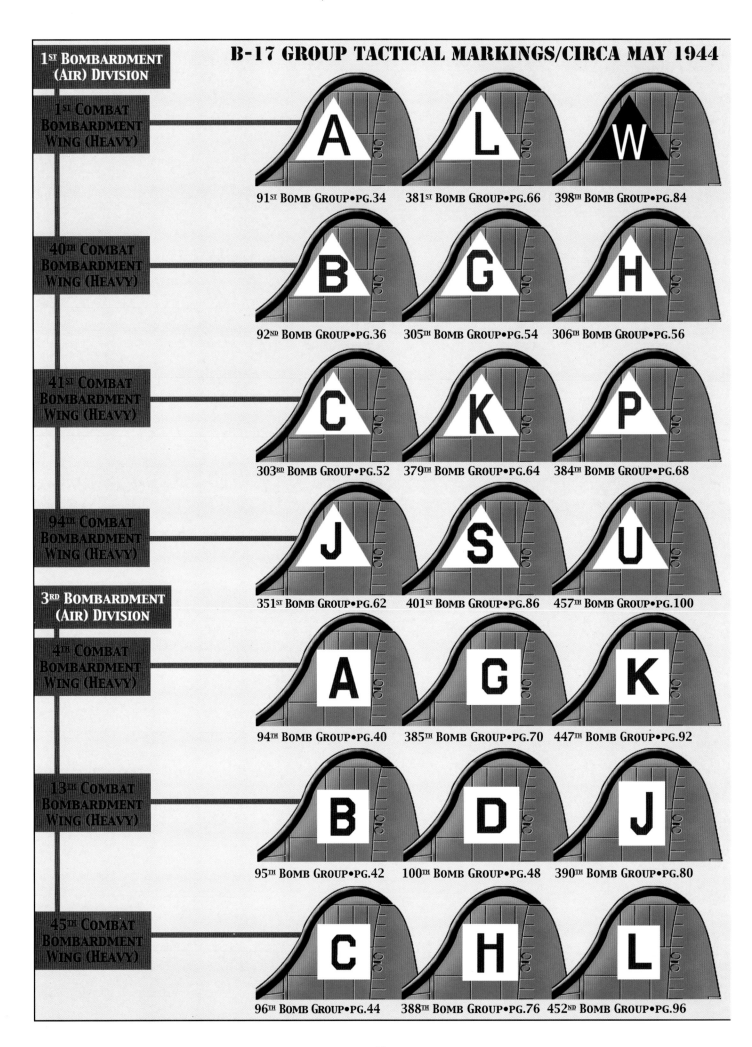

B-17 GROUP TACTICAL MARKINGS/CIRCA MAY 1944

1ST BOMBARDMENT (AIR) DIVISION

1ST COMBAT BOMBARDMENT WING (HEAVY)

A — 91ST BOMB GROUP•PG.34
L — 381ST BOMB GROUP•PG.66
W — 398TH BOMB GROUP•PG.84

40TH COMBAT BOMBARDMENT WING (HEAVY)

B — 92ND BOMB GROUP•PG.36
G — 305TH BOMB GROUP•PG.54
H — 306TH BOMB GROUP•PG.56

41ST COMBAT BOMBARDMENT WING (HEAVY)

C — 303RD BOMB GROUP•PG.52
K — 379TH BOMB GROUP•PG.64
P — 384TH BOMB GROUP•PG.68

94TH COMBAT BOMBARDMENT WING (HEAVY)

J — 351ST BOMB GROUP•PG.62
S — 401ST BOMB GROUP•PG.86
U — 457TH BOMB GROUP•PG.100

3RD BOMBARDMENT (AIR) DIVISION

4TH COMBAT BOMBARDMENT WING (HEAVY)

A — 94TH BOMB GROUP•PG.40
G — 385TH BOMB GROUP•PG.70
K — 447TH BOMB GROUP•PG.92

13TH COMBAT BOMBARDMENT WING (HEAVY)

B — 95TH BOMB GROUP•PG.42
D — 100TH BOMB GROUP•PG.48
J — 390TH BOMB GROUP•PG.80

45TH COMBAT BOMBARDMENT WING (HEAVY)

C — 96TH BOMB GROUP•PG.44
H — 388TH BOMB GROUP•PG.76
L — 452ND BOMB GROUP•PG.96

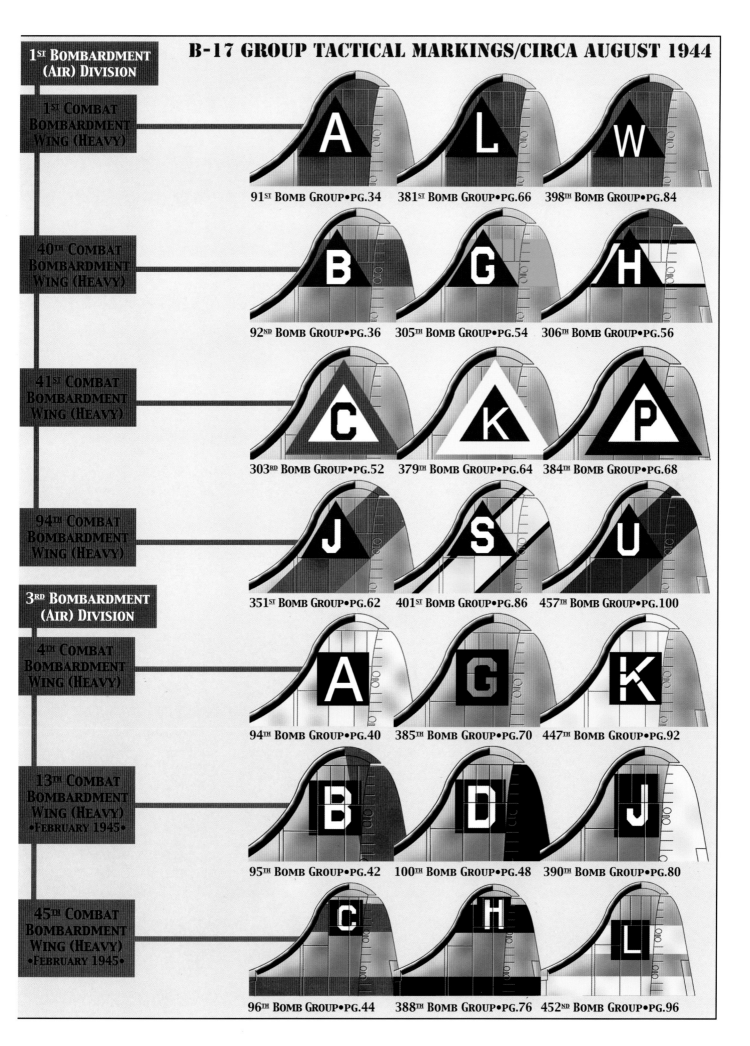

1ST BOMBARDMENT (AIR) DIVISION

B-17 GROUP TACTICAL MARKINGS/CIRCA AUGUST 1944

1ST COMBAT BOMBARDMENT WING (HEAVY)

A — 91ST BOMB GROUP•PG.34
L — 381ST BOMB GROUP•PG.66
W — 398TH BOMB GROUP•PG.84

40TH COMBAT BOMBARDMENT WING (HEAVY)

B — 92ND BOMB GROUP•PG.36
G — 305TH BOMB GROUP•PG.54
H — 306TH BOMB GROUP•PG.56

41ST COMBAT BOMBARDMENT WING (HEAVY)

C — 303RD BOMB GROUP•PG.52
K — 379TH BOMB GROUP•PG.64
P — 384TH BOMB GROUP•PG.68

94TH COMBAT BOMBARDMENT WING (HEAVY)

J — 351ST BOMB GROUP•PG.62
S — 401ST BOMB GROUP•PG.86
U — 457TH BOMB GROUP•PG.100

3RD BOMBARDMENT (AIR) DIVISION

4TH COMBAT BOMBARDMENT WING (HEAVY)

A — 94TH BOMB GROUP•PG.40
G — 385TH BOMB GROUP•PG.70
K — 447TH BOMB GROUP•PG.92

13TH COMBAT BOMBARDMENT WING (HEAVY) •FEBRUARY 1945•

B — 95TH BOMB GROUP•PG.42
D — 100TH BOMB GROUP•PG.48
J — 390TH BOMB GROUP•PG.80

45TH COMBAT BOMBARDMENT WING (HEAVY) •FEBRUARY 1945•

C — 96TH BOMB GROUP•PG.44
H — 388TH BOMB GROUP•PG.76
L — 452ND BOMB GROUP•PG.96

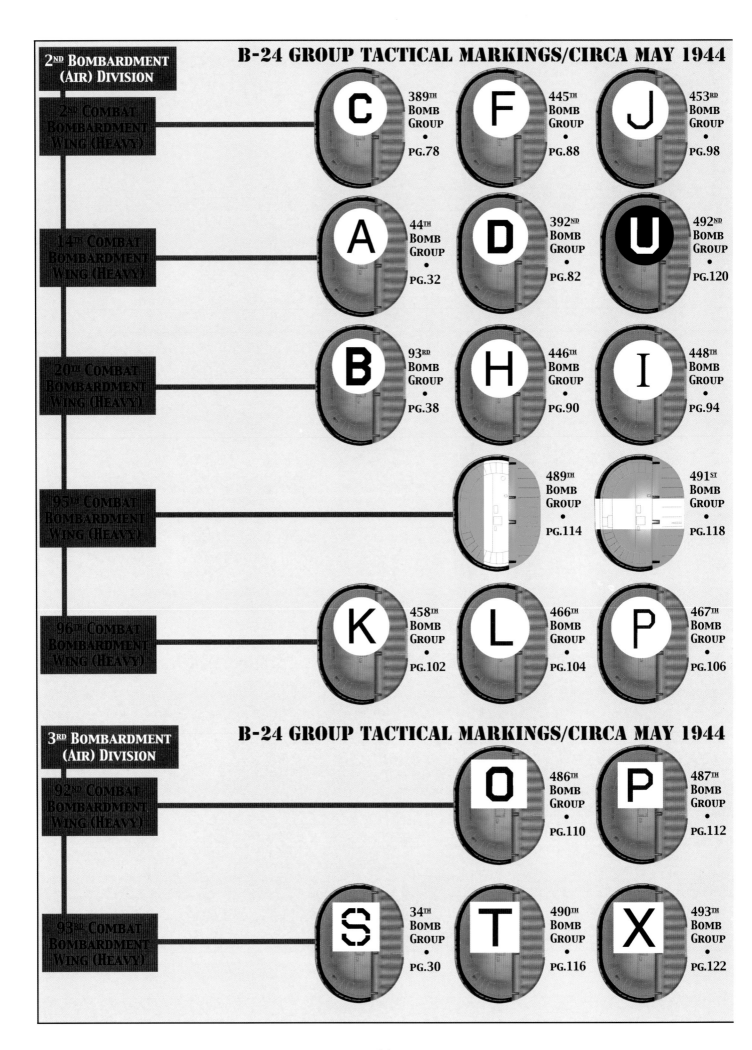

2ND BOMBARDMENT (AIR) DIVISION

2ND COMBAT BOMBARDMENT WING (HEAVY)

14TH COMBAT BOMBARDMENT WING (HEAVY)

20TH COMBAT BOMBARDMENT WING (HEAVY)

95TH COMBAT BOMBARDMENT WING (HEAVY)

96TH COMBAT BOMBARDMENT WING (HEAVY)

3RD BOMBARDMENT (AIR) DIVISION

92ND COMBAT BOMBARDMENT WING (HEAVY)

93RD COMBAT BOMBARDMENT WING (HEAVY)

B-24 GROUP TACTICAL MARKINGS/CIRCA MAY 1944

C — 389TH BOMB GROUP • PG.78

F — 445TH BOMB GROUP • PG.88

J — 453RD BOMB GROUP • PG.98

A — 44TH BOMB GROUP • PG.32

D — 392ND BOMB GROUP • PG.82

U — 492ND BOMB GROUP • PG.120

B — 93RD BOMB GROUP • PG.38

H — 446TH BOMB GROUP • PG.90

I — 448TH BOMB GROUP • PG.94

489TH BOMB GROUP • PG.114

491ST BOMB GROUP • PG.118

K — 458TH BOMB GROUP • PG.102

L — 466TH BOMB GROUP • PG.104

P — 467TH BOMB GROUP • PG.106

B-24 GROUP TACTICAL MARKINGS/CIRCA MAY 1944

O — 486TH BOMB GROUP • PG.110

P — 487TH BOMB GROUP • PG.112

S — 34TH BOMB GROUP • PG.30

T — 490TH BOMB GROUP • PG.116

X — 493RD BOMB GROUP • PG.122

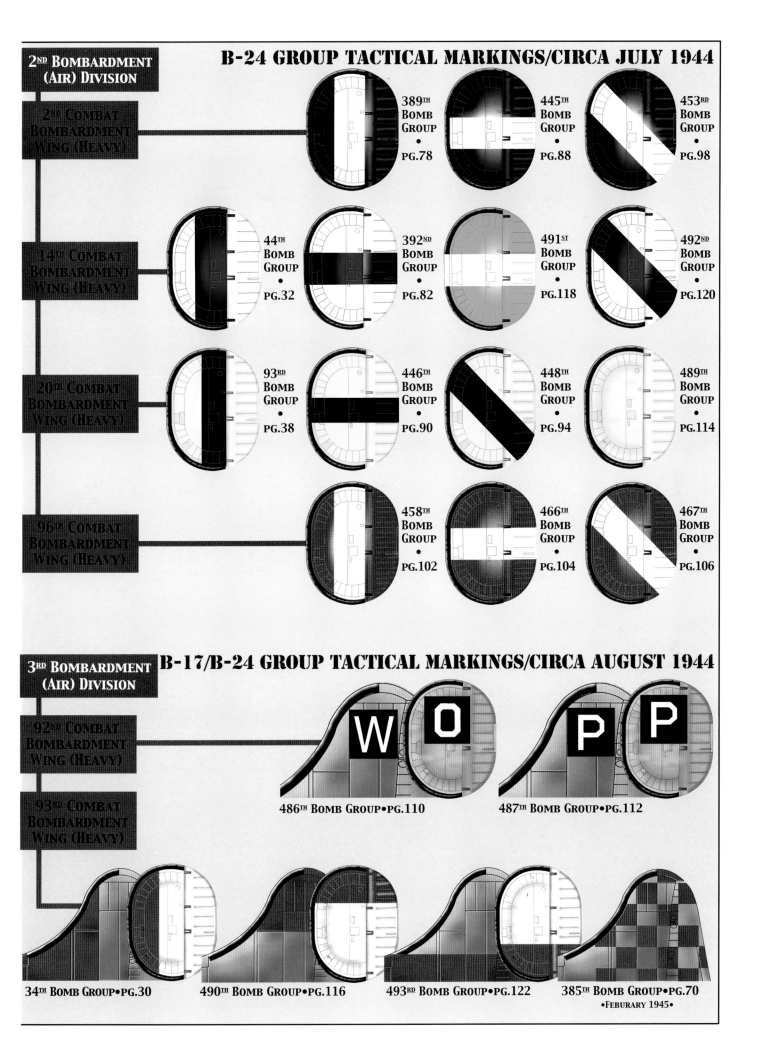

2ND BOMBARDMENT (AIR) DIVISION

2ND COMBAT BOMBARDMENT WING (HEAVY)

14TH COMBAT BOMBARDMENT WING (HEAVY)

20TH COMBAT BOMBARDMENT WING (HEAVY)

96TH COMBAT BOMBARDMENT WING (HEAVY)

B-24 GROUP TACTICAL MARKINGS/CIRCA JULY 1944

389TH BOMB GROUP • PG.78

445TH BOMB GROUP • PG.88

453RD BOMB GROUP • PG.98

44TH BOMB GROUP • PG.32

392ND BOMB GROUP • PG.82

491ST BOMB GROUP • PG.118

492ND BOMB GROUP • PG.120

93RD BOMB GROUP • PG.38

446TH BOMB GROUP • PG.90

448TH BOMB GROUP • PG.94

489TH BOMB GROUP • PG.114

458TH BOMB GROUP • PG.102

466TH BOMB GROUP • PG.104

467TH BOMB GROUP • PG.106

3RD BOMBARDMENT (AIR) DIVISION

92ND COMBAT BOMBARDMENT WING (HEAVY)

93RD COMBAT BOMBARDMENT WING (HEAVY)

B-17/B-24 GROUP TACTICAL MARKINGS/CIRCA AUGUST 1944

486TH BOMB GROUP • PG.110

487TH BOMB GROUP • PG.112

34TH BOMB GROUP • PG.30

490TH BOMB GROUP • PG.116

493RD BOMB GROUP • PG.122

385TH BOMB GROUP • PG.70
• FEBURARY 1945 •

34TH BOMB GROUP	4TH BMB SQDN	7TH BMB SQDN	18TH BMB SQDN	391ST BMB SQDN
44TH BOMB GROUP	66TH BMB SQDN	67TH BMB SQDN	68TH BMB SQDN	506TH BMB SQDN
91ST BOMB GROUP	322ND BMB SQDN	323RD BMB SQDN	324TH BMB SQDN	401ST BMB SQDN
92ND BOMB GROUP	325TH BMB SQDN	326TH BMB SQDN	327TH BMB SQDN	407TH BMB SQDN
93RD BOMB GROUP	328TH BMB SQDN	329TH BMB SQDN	330TH BMB SQDN	409TH BMB SQDN
94TH BOMB GROUP	331ST BMB SQDN	332ND BMB SQDN	333RD BMB SQDN	410TH BMB SQDN
95TH BOMB GROUP	334TH BMB SQDN	335TH BMB SQDN	336TH BMB SQDN	412TH BMB SQDN
96TH BOMB GROUP	337TH BMB SQDN	338TH BMB SQDN	339TH BMB SQDN	413TH BMB SQDN
97TH BOMB GROUP	340TH BMB SQDN	341ST BMB SQDN	342ND BMB SQDN	414TH BMB SQDN
100TH BOMB GROUP	349TH BMB SQDN	350TH BMB SQDN	351ST BMB SQDN	418TH BMB SQDN
301ST BOMB GROUP	32ND BMB SQDN	352ND BMB SQDN	353RD BMB SQDN	419TH BMB SQDN
303RD BOMB GROUP	358TH BMB SQDN	359TH BMB SQDN	360TH BMB SQDN	427TH BMB SQDN
305TH BOMB GROUP	364TH BMB SQDN	365TH BMB SQDN	366TH BMB SQDN	422ND BMB SQDN
306TH BOMB GROUP	367TH BMB SQDN	368TH BMB SQDN	369TH BMB SQDN	423RD BMB SQDN
322ND BOMB GROUP	449TH BMB SQDN	450TH BMB SQDN	451ST BMB SQDN	452ND BMB SQDN
323RD BOMB GROUP	453RD BMB SQDN	454TH BMB SQDN	455TH BMB SQDN	456TH BMB SQDN
351ST BOMB GROUP	508TH BMB SQDN	509TH BMB SQDN	510TH BMB SQDN	511TH BMB SQDN
379TH BOMB GROUP	524TH BMB SQDN	525TH BMB SQDN	526TH BMB SQDN	527TH BMB SQDN
381ST BOMB GROUP	532ND BMB SQDN	533RD BMB SQDN	534TH BMB SQDN	535TH BMB SQDN
384TH BOMB GROUP	544TH BMB SQDN	545TH BMB SQDN	546TH BMB SQDN	547TH BMB SQDN
385TH BOMB GROUP	548TH BMB SQDN	549TH BMB SQDN	550TH BMB SQDN	551ST BMB SQDN
386TH BOMB GROUP	552ND BMB SQDN	553RD BMB SQDN	554TH BMB SQDN	555TH BMB SQDN

387th Bomb Group	556th Bmb Sqdn	557th Bmb Sqdn	558th Bmb Sqdn	559th Bmb Sqdn
388th Bomb Group	560th Bmb Sqdn	561st Bmb Sqdn	562nd Bmb Sqdn	563rd Bmb Sqdn
389th Bomb Group	564th Bmb Sqdn	565th Bmb Sqdn	566th Bmb Sqdn	567th Bmb Sqdn
390th Bomb Group	568th Bmb Sqdn	569th Bmb Sqdn	570th Bmb Sqdn	571st Bmb Sqdn
392nd Bomb Group	576th Bmb Sqdn	577th Bmb Sqdn	578th Bmb Sqdn	579th Bmb Sqdn
398th Bomb Group	600th Bmb Sqdn	601st Bmb Sqdn	602nd Bmb Sqdn	603rd Bmb Sqdn
401st Bomb Group	612th Bmb Sqdn	613th Bmb Sqdn	614th Bmb Sqdn	615th Bmb Sqdn
445th Bomb Group	700th Bmb Sqdn	701st Bmb Sqdn	702nd Bmb Sqdn	703rd Bmb Sqdn
446th Bomb Group	704th Bmb Sqdn	705th Bmb Sqdn	706th Bmb Sqdn	707th Bmb Sqdn
447th Bomb Group	708th Bmb Sqdn	709th Bmb Sqdn	710th Bmb Sqdn	711th Bmb Sqdn
448th Bomb Group	712th Bmb Sqdn	713th Bmb Sqdn	714th Bmb Sqdn	715th Bmb Sqdn
452nd Bomb Group	728th Bmb Sqdn	729th Bmb Sqdn	730th Bmb Sqdn	731st Bmb Sqdn
453rd Bomb Group	732nd Bmb Sqdn	733rd Bmb Sqdn	734th Bmb Sqdn	735th Bmb Sqdn
457th Bomb Group	748th Bmb Sqdn	749th Bmb Sqdn	750th Bmb Sqdn	751st Bmb Sqdn
458th Bomb Group	752nd Bmb Sqdn	753rd Bmb Sqdn	754th Bmb Sqdn	755th Bmb Sqdn
466th Bomb Group	784th Bmb Sqdn	785th Bmb Sqdn	786th Bmb Sqdn	787th Bmb Sqdn
467th Bomb Group	788th Bmb Sqdn	789th Bmb Sqdn	790th Bmb Sqdn	791st Bmb Sqdn
482nd Bomb Group	812th Bmb Sqdn	813th Bmb Sqdn	814th Bmb Sqdn	406th Bmb Sqdn
486th Bomb Group	832nd Bmb Sqdn	833rd Bmb Sqdn	834th Bmb Sqdn	835th Bmb Sqdn
487th Bomb Group	836th Bmb Sqdn	837th Bmb Sqdn	838th Bmb Sqdn	839th Bmb Sqdn
489th Bomb Group	844th Bmb Sqdn	845th Bmb Sqdn	846th Bmb Sqdn	847th Bmb Sqdn
490th Bomb Group	848th Bmb Sqdn	849th Bmb Sqdn	850th Bmb Sqdn	851st Bmb Sqdn
491st Bomb Group	852nd Bmb Sqdn	853rd Bmb Sqdn	854th Bmb Sqdn	855th Bmb Sqdn
492nd Bomb Group	406th Bmb Sqdn	856th Bmb Sqdn	857th Bmb Sqdn	858th Bmb Sqdn
493rd Bomb Group	860th Bmb Sqdn	861st Bmb Sqdn	862nd Bmb Sqdn	863rd Bmb Sqdn

ORGANIZATION & DEPLOYMENT
EIGHTH AAF/(VIII) BOMBER COMMAND

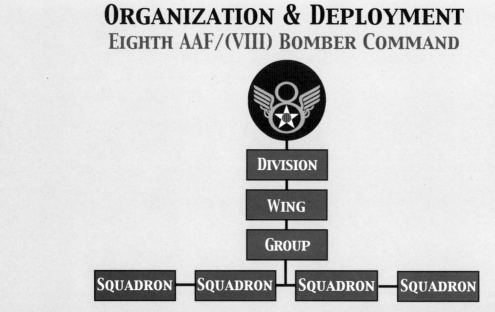

DIVISION

WING

GROUP

SQUADRON — SQUADRON — SQUADRON — SQUADRON

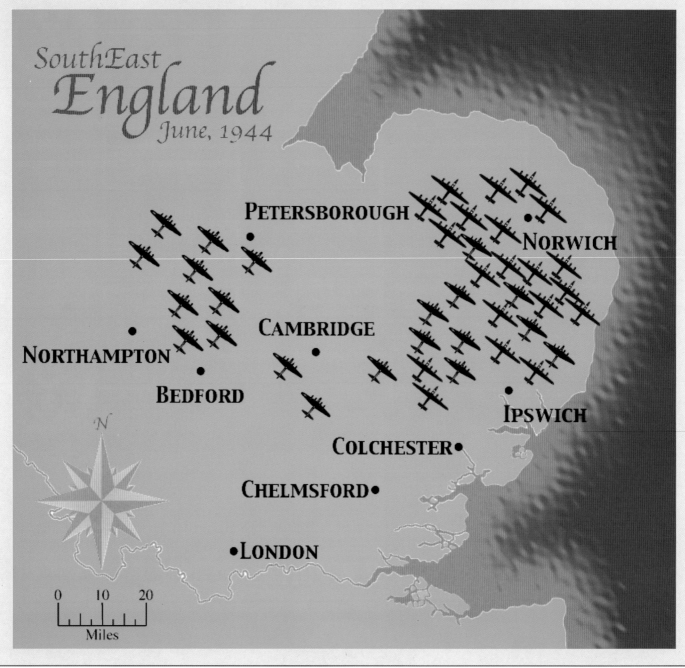

SouthEast
England
June, 1944

PETERSBOROUGH

NORWICH

CAMBRIDGE

NORTHAMPTON

BEDFORD

N

IPSWICH

COLCHESTER

CHELMSFORD

• LONDON

0   10   20
Miles

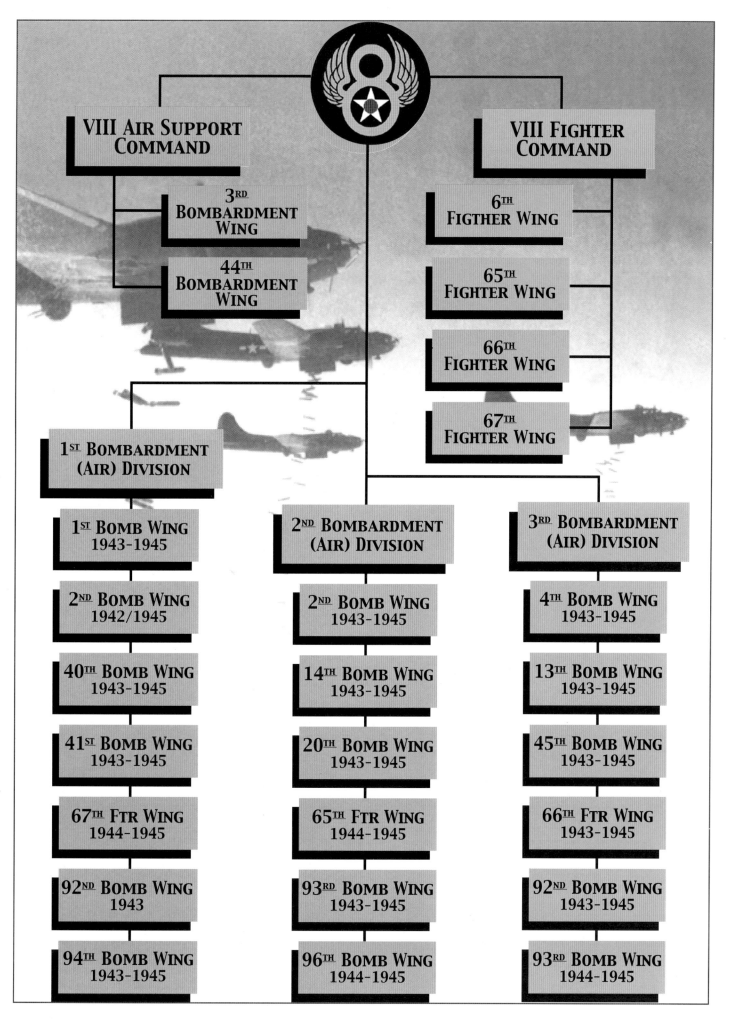

VIII Air Support Command

- 3rd Bombardment Wing
- 44th Bombardment Wing

VIII Fighter Command

- 6th Figther Wing
- 65th Fighter Wing
- 66th Fighter Wing
- 67th Fighter Wing

1st Bombardment (Air) Division

- 1st Bomb Wing 1943-1945
- 2nd Bomb Wing 1942/1945
- 40th Bomb Wing 1943-1945
- 41st Bomb Wing 1943-1945
- 67th Ftr Wing 1944-1945
- 92nd Bomb Wing 1943
- 94th Bomb Wing 1943-1945

2nd Bombardment (Air) Division

- 2nd Bomb Wing 1943-1945
- 14th Bomb Wing 1943-1945
- 20th Bomb Wing 1943-1945
- 65th Ftr Wing 1944-1945
- 93rd Bomb Wing 1943-1945
- 96th Bomb Wing 1944-1945

3rd Bombardment (Air) Division

- 4th Bomb Wing 1943-1945
- 13th Bomb Wing 1943-1945
- 45th Bomb Wing 1943-1945
- 66th Ftr Wing 1943-1945
- 92nd Bomb Wing 1943-1945
- 93rd Bomb Wing 1944-1945

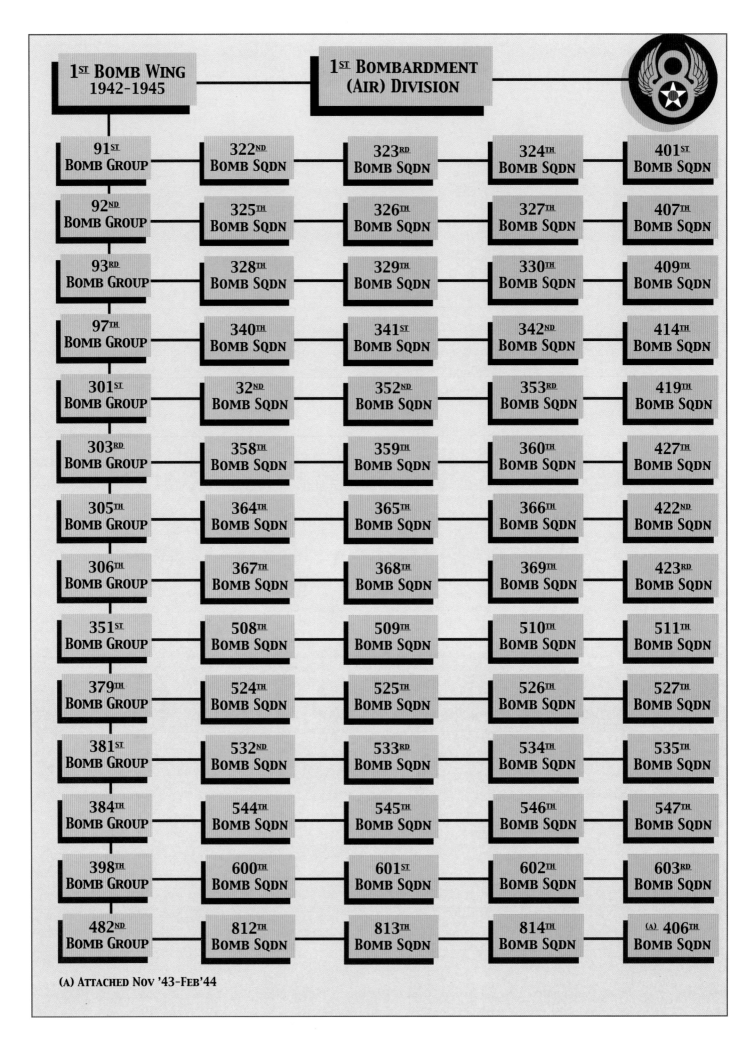

1ST BOMB WING 1942-1945	**1ST BOMBARDMENT (AIR) DIVISION**			
91ST BOMB GROUP	**322ND BOMB SQDN**	**323RD BOMB SQDN**	**324TH BOMB SQDN**	**401ST BOMB SQDN**
92ND BOMB GROUP	**325TH BOMB SQDN**	**326TH BOMB SQDN**	**327TH BOMB SQDN**	**407TH BOMB SQDN**
93RD BOMB GROUP	**328TH BOMB SQDN**	**329TH BOMB SQDN**	**330TH BOMB SQDN**	**409TH BOMB SQDN**
97TH BOMB GROUP	**340TH BOMB SQDN**	**341ST BOMB SQDN**	**342ND BOMB SQDN**	**414TH BOMB SQDN**
301ST BOMB GROUP	**32ND BOMB SQDN**	**352ND BOMB SQDN**	**353RD BOMB SQDN**	**419TH BOMB SQDN**
303RD BOMB GROUP	**358TH BOMB SQDN**	**359TH BOMB SQDN**	**360TH BOMB SQDN**	**427TH BOMB SQDN**
305TH BOMB GROUP	**364TH BOMB SQDN**	**365TH BOMB SQDN**	**366TH BOMB SQDN**	**422ND BOMB SQDN**
306TH BOMB GROUP	**367TH BOMB SQDN**	**368TH BOMB SQDN**	**369TH BOMB SQDN**	**423RD BOMB SQDN**
351ST BOMB GROUP	**508TH BOMB SQDN**	**509TH BOMB SQDN**	**510TH BOMB SQDN**	**511TH BOMB SQDN**
379TH BOMB GROUP	**524TH BOMB SQDN**	**525TH BOMB SQDN**	**526TH BOMB SQDN**	**527TH BOMB SQDN**
381ST BOMB GROUP	**532ND BOMB SQDN**	**533RD BOMB SQDN**	**534TH BOMB SQDN**	**535TH BOMB SQDN**
384TH BOMB GROUP	**544TH BOMB SQDN**	**545TH BOMB SQDN**	**546TH BOMB SQDN**	**547TH BOMB SQDN**
398TH BOMB GROUP	**600TH BOMB SQDN**	**601ST BOMB SQDN**	**602TH BOMB SQDN**	**603RD BOMB SQDN**
482ND BOMB GROUP	**812TH BOMB SQDN**	**813TH BOMB SQDN**	**814TH BOMB SQDN**	**(A) 406TH BOMB SQDN**

(A) ATTACHED NOV '43-FEB '44

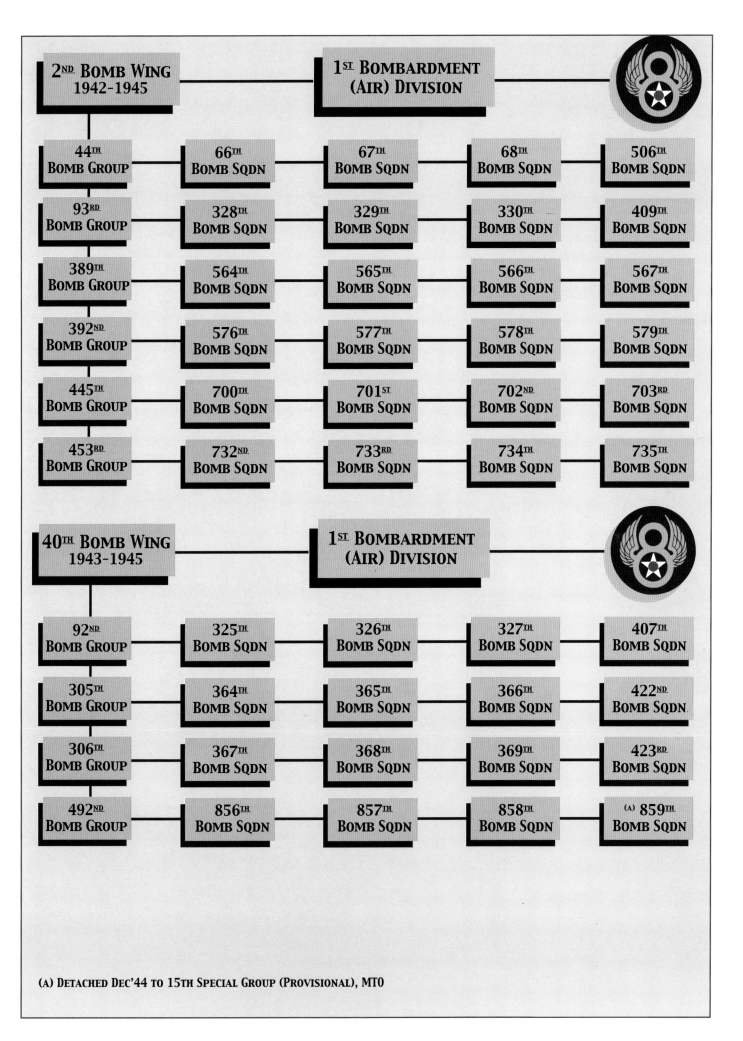

2ND BOMB WING 1942-1945 — **1ST BOMBARDMENT (AIR) DIVISION**

44TH BOMB GROUP	66TH BOMB SQDN	67TH BOMB SQDN	68TH BOMB SQDN	506TH BOMB SQDN
93RD BOMB GROUP	328TH BOMB SQDN	329TH BOMB SQDN	330TH BOMB SQDN	409TH BOMB SQDN
389TH BOMB GROUP	564TH BOMB SQDN	565TH BOMB SQDN	566TH BOMB SQDN	567TH BOMB SQDN
392ND BOMB GROUP	576TH BOMB SQDN	577TH BOMB SQDN	578TH BOMB SQDN	579TH BOMB SQDN
445TH BOMB GROUP	700TH BOMB SQDN	701ST BOMB SQDN	702ND BOMB SQDN	703RD BOMB SQDN
453RD BOMB GROUP	732ND BOMB SQDN	733RD BOMB SQDN	734TH BOMB SQDN	735TH BOMB SQDN

40TH BOMB WING 1943-1945 — **1ST BOMBARDMENT (AIR) DIVISION**

92ND BOMB GROUP	325TH BOMB SQDN	326TH BOMB SQDN	327TH BOMB SQDN	407TH BOMB SQDN
305TH BOMB GROUP	364TH BOMB SQDN	365TH BOMB SQDN	366TH BOMB SQDN	422ND BOMB SQDN
306TH BOMB GROUP	367TH BOMB SQDN	368TH BOMB SQDN	369TH BOMB SQDN	423RD BOMB SQDN
492ND BOMB GROUP	856TH BOMB SQDN	857TH BOMB SQDN	858TH BOMB SQDN	(A) 859TH BOMB SQDN

(A) DETACHED DEC'44 TO 15TH SPECIAL GROUP (PROVISIONAL), MTO

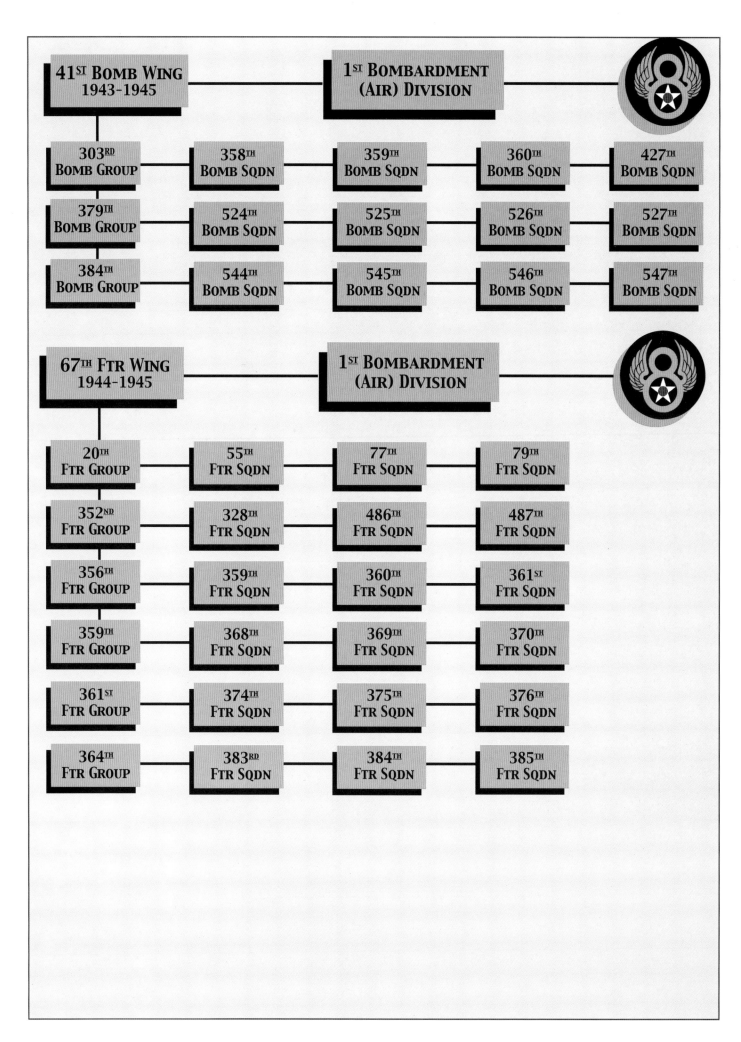

41ST BOMB WING 1943-1945 — **1ST BOMBARDMENT (AIR) DIVISION**

- **303RD BOMB GROUP** — 358TH BOMB SQDN — 359TH BOMB SQDN — 360TH BOMB SQDN — 427TH BOMB SQDN
- **379TH BOMB GROUP** — 524TH BOMB SQDN — 525TH BOMB SQDN — 526TH BOMB SQDN — 527TH BOMB SQDN
- **384TH BOMB GROUP** — 544TH BOMB SQDN — 545TH BOMB SQDN — 546TH BOMB SQDN — 547TH BOMB SQDN

67TH FTR WING 1944-1945 — **1ST BOMBARDMENT (AIR) DIVISION**

- **20TH FTR GROUP** — 55TH FTR SQDN — 77TH FTR SQDN — 79TH FTR SQDN
- **352ND FTR GROUP** — 328TH FTR SQDN — 486TH FTR SQDN — 487TH FTR SQDN
- **356TH FTR GROUP** — 359TH FTR SQDN — 360TH FTR SQDN — 361ST FTR SQDN
- **359TH FTR GROUP** — 368TH FTR SQDN — 369TH FTR SQDN — 370TH FTR SQDN
- **361ST FTR GROUP** — 374TH FTR SQDN — 375TH FTR SQDN — 376TH FTR SQDN
- **364TH FTR GROUP** — 383RD FTR SQDN — 384TH FTR SQDN — 385TH FTR SQDN

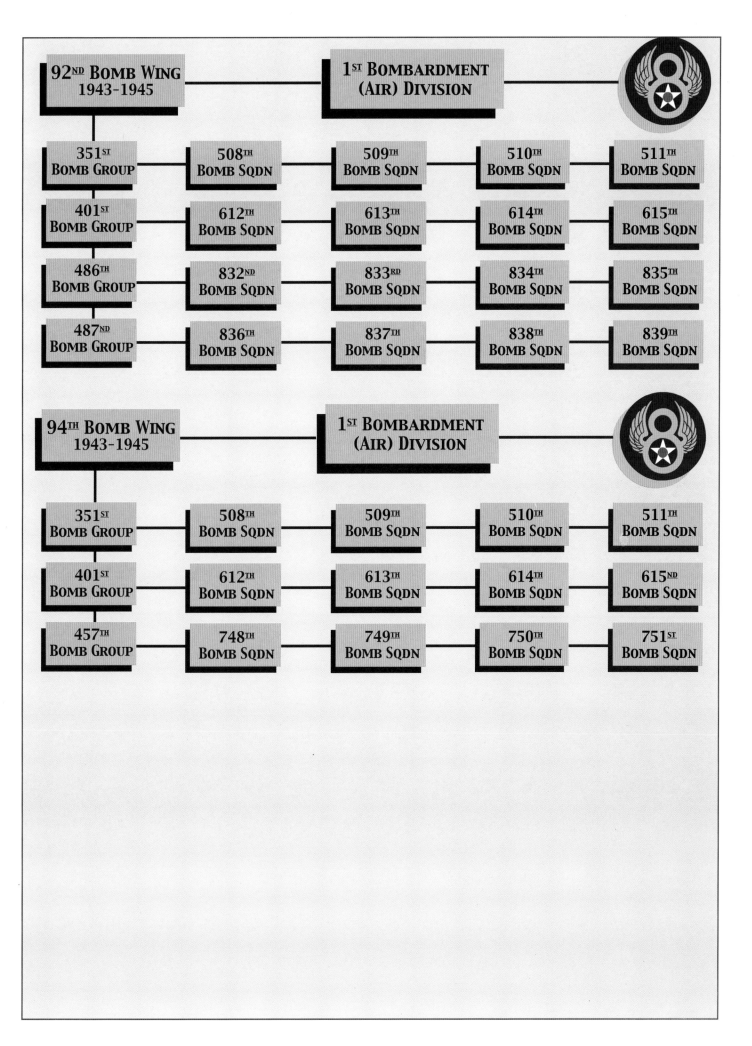

92ND BOMB WING 1943-1945 — **1ST BOMBARDMENT (AIR) DIVISION**

- **351ST BOMB GROUP** — 508TH BOMB SQDN — 509TH BOMB SQDN — 510TH BOMB SQDN — 511TH BOMB SQDN
- **401ST BOMB GROUP** — 612TH BOMB SQDN — 613TH BOMB SQDN — 614TH BOMB SQDN — 615TH BOMB SQDN
- **486TH BOMB GROUP** — 832ND BOMB SQDN — 833RD BOMB SQDN — 834TH BOMB SQDN — 835TH BOMB SQDN
- **487ND BOMB GROUP** — 836TH BOMB SQDN — 837TH BOMB SQDN — 838TH BOMB SQDN — 839TH BOMB SQDN

94TH BOMB WING 1943-1945 — **1ST BOMBARDMENT (AIR) DIVISION**

- **351ST BOMB GROUP** — 508TH BOMB SQDN — 509TH BOMB SQDN — 510TH BOMB SQDN — 511TH BOMB SQDN
- **401ST BOMB GROUP** — 612TH BOMB SQDN — 613TH BOMB SQDN — 614TH BOMB SQDN — 615ND BOMB SQDN
- **457TH BOMB GROUP** — 748TH BOMB SQDN — 749TH BOMB SQDN — 750TH BOMB SQDN — 751ST BOMB SQDN

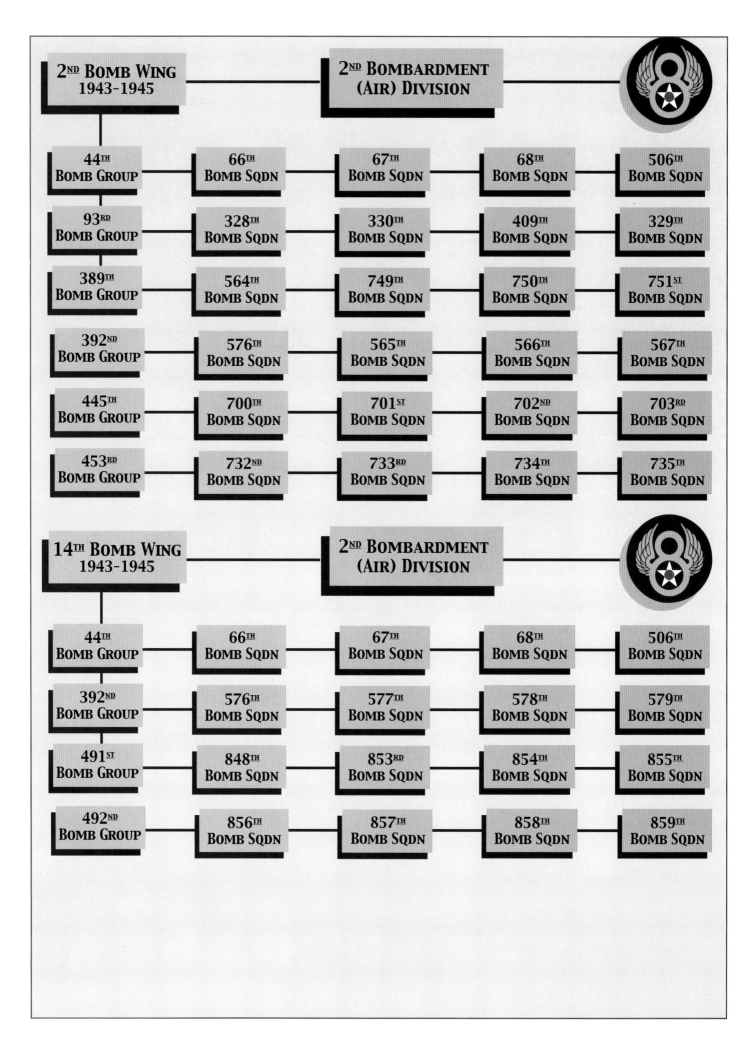

2ND BOMB WING
1943-1945

2ND BOMBARDMENT
(AIR) DIVISION

44TH BOMB GROUP	66TH BOMB SQDN	67TH BOMB SQDN	68TH BOMB SQDN	506TH BOMB SQDN
93RD BOMB GROUP	328TH BOMB SQDN	330TH BOMB SQDN	409TH BOMB SQDN	329TH BOMB SQDN
389TH BOMB GROUP	564TH BOMB SQDN	749TH BOMB SQDN	750TH BOMB SQDN	751ST BOMB SQDN
392ND BOMB GROUP	576TH BOMB SQDN	565TH BOMB SQDN	566TH BOMB SQDN	567TH BOMB SQDN
445TH BOMB GROUP	700TH BOMB SQDN	701ST BOMB SQDN	702ND BOMB SQDN	703RD BOMB SQDN
453RD BOMB GROUP	732ND BOMB SQDN	733RD BOMB SQDN	734TH BOMB SQDN	735TH BOMB SQDN

14TH BOMB WING
1943-1945

2ND BOMBARDMENT
(AIR) DIVISION

44TH BOMB GROUP	66TH BOMB SQDN	67TH BOMB SQDN	68TH BOMB SQDN	506TH BOMB SQDN
392ND BOMB GROUP	576TH BOMB SQDN	577TH BOMB SQDN	578TH BOMB SQDN	579TH BOMB SQDN
491ST BOMB GROUP	848TH BOMB SQDN	853RD BOMB SQDN	854TH BOMB SQDN	855TH BOMB SQDN
492ND BOMB GROUP	856TH BOMB SQDN	857TH BOMB SQDN	858TH BOMB SQDN	859TH BOMB SQDN

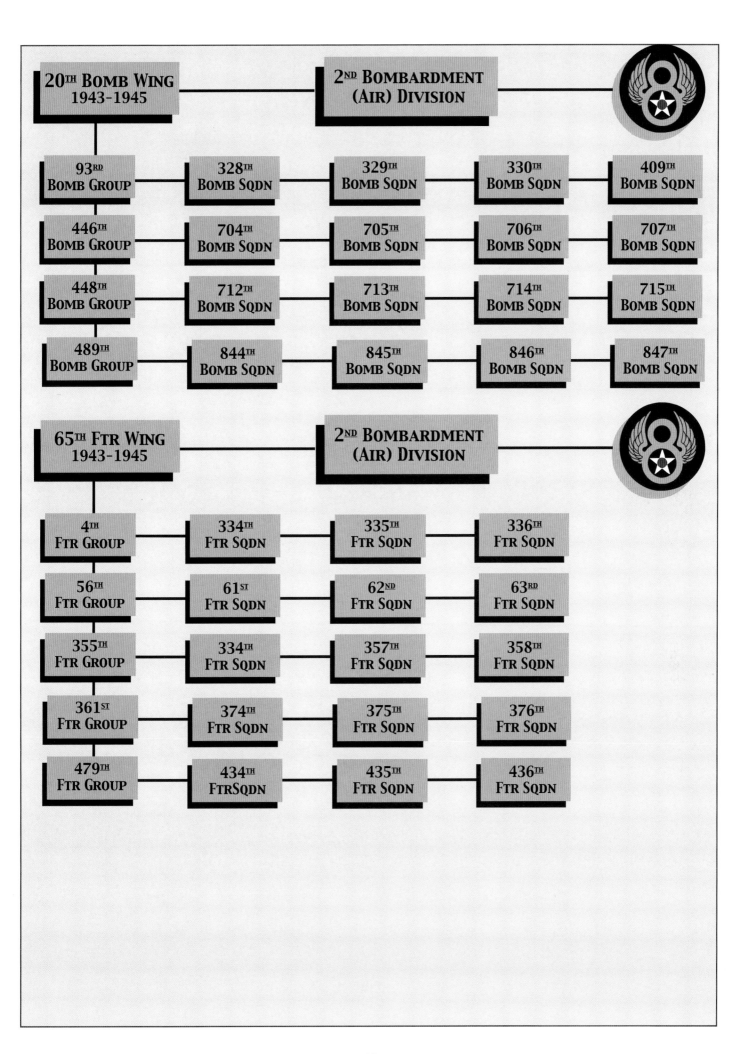

20TH BOMB WING 1943-1945 — **2ND BOMBARDMENT (AIR) DIVISION**

- **93RD BOMB GROUP** — **328TH BOMB SQDN** — **329TH BOMB SQDN** — **330TH BOMB SQDN** — **409TH BOMB SQDN**
- **446TH BOMB GROUP** — **704TH BOMB SQDN** — **705TH BOMB SQDN** — **706TH BOMB SQDN** — **707TH BOMB SQDN**
- **448TH BOMB GROUP** — **712TH BOMB SQDN** — **713TH BOMB SQDN** — **714TH BOMB SQDN** — **715TH BOMB SQDN**
- **489TH BOMB GROUP** — **844TH BOMB SQDN** — **845TH BOMB SQDN** — **846TH BOMB SQDN** — **847TH BOMB SQDN**

65TH FTR WING 1943-1945 — **2ND BOMBARDMENT (AIR) DIVISION**

- **4TH FTR GROUP** — **334TH FTR SQDN** — **335TH FTR SQDN** — **336TH FTR SQDN**
- **56TH FTR GROUP** — **61ST FTR SQDN** — **62ND FTR SQDN** — **63RD FTR SQDN**
- **355TH FTR GROUP** — **334TH FTR SQDN** — **357TH FTR SQDN** — **358TH FTR SQDN**
- **361ST FTR GROUP** — **374TH FTR SQDN** — **375TH FTR SQDN** — **376TH FTR SQDN**
- **479TH FTR GROUP** — **434TH FTRSQDN** — **435TH FTR SQDN** — **436TH FTR SQDN**

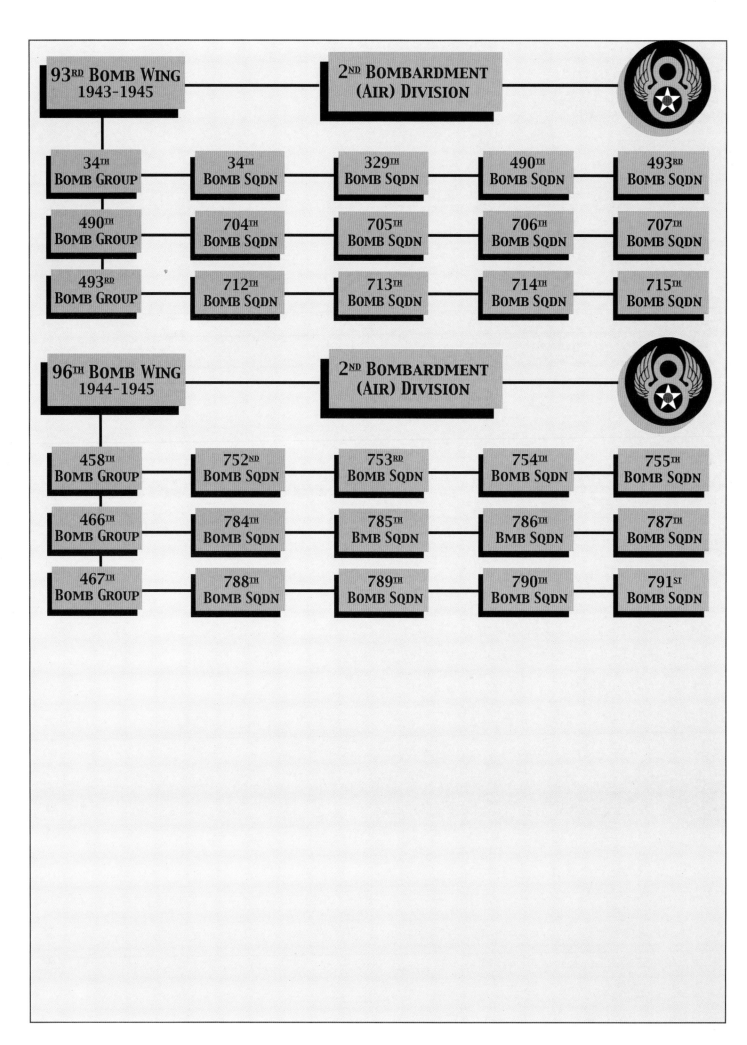

93RD BOMB WING 1943-1945 — **2ND BOMBARDMENT (AIR) DIVISION**

34TH BOMB GROUP	34TH BOMB SQDN	329TH BOMB SQDN	490TH BOMB SQDN	493RD BOMB SQDN
490TH BOMB GROUP	704TH BOMB SQDN	705TH BOMB SQDN	706TH BOMB SQDN	707TH BOMB SQDN
493RD BOMB GROUP	712TH BOMB SQDN	713TH BOMB SQDN	714TH BOMB SQDN	715TH BOMB SQDN

96TH BOMB WING 1944-1945 — **2ND BOMBARDMENT (AIR) DIVISION**

458TH BOMB GROUP	752ND BOMB SQDN	753RD BOMB SQDN	754TH BOMB SQDN	755TH BOMB SQDN
466TH BOMB GROUP	784TH BOMB SQDN	785TH BMB SQDN	786TH BMB SQDN	787TH BOMB SQDN
467TH BOMB GROUP	788TH BOMB SQDN	789TH BOMB SQDN	790TH BOMB SQDN	791ST BOMB SQDN

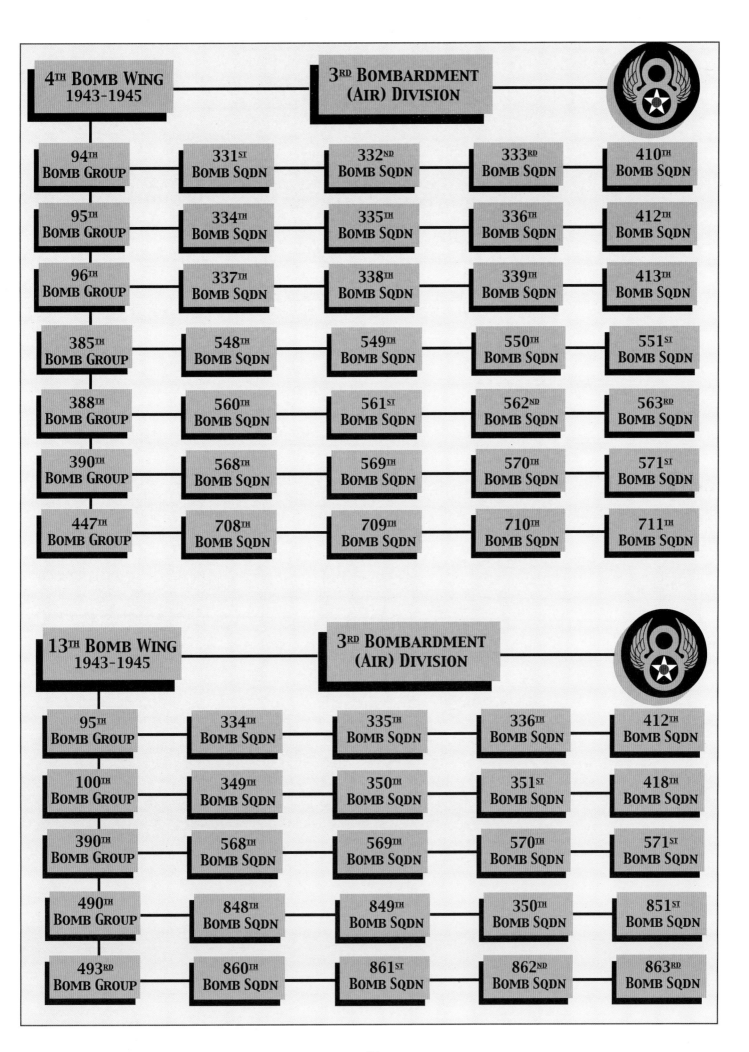

4TH BOMB WING 1943-1945 — **3RD BOMBARDMENT (AIR) DIVISION**

94TH BOMB GROUP	331ST BOMB SQDN	332ND BOMB SQDN	333RD BOMB SQDN	410TH BOMB SQDN
95TH BOMB GROUP	334TH BOMB SQDN	335TH BOMB SQDN	336TH BOMB SQDN	412TH BOMB SQDN
96TH BOMB GROUP	337TH BOMB SQDN	338TH BOMB SQDN	339TH BOMB SQDN	413TH BOMB SQDN
385TH BOMB GROUP	548TH BOMB SQDN	549TH BOMB SQDN	550TH BOMB SQDN	551ST BOMB SQDN
388TH BOMB GROUP	560TH BOMB SQDN	561ST BOMB SQDN	562ND BOMB SQDN	563RD BOMB SQDN
390TH BOMB GROUP	568TH BOMB SQDN	569TH BOMB SQDN	570TH BOMB SQDN	571ST BOMB SQDN
447TH BOMB GROUP	708TH BOMB SQDN	709TH BOMB SQDN	710TH BOMB SQDN	711TH BOMB SQDN

13TH BOMB WING 1943-1945 — **3RD BOMBARDMENT (AIR) DIVISION**

95TH BOMB GROUP	334TH BOMB SQDN	335TH BOMB SQDN	336TH BOMB SQDN	412TH BOMB SQDN
100TH BOMB GROUP	349TH BOMB SQDN	350TH BOMB SQDN	351ST BOMB SQDN	418TH BOMB SQDN
390TH BOMB GROUP	568TH BOMB SQDN	569TH BOMB SQDN	570TH BOMB SQDN	571ST BOMB SQDN
490TH BOMB GROUP	848TH BOMB SQDN	849TH BOMB SQDN	350TH BOMB SQDN	851ST BOMB SQDN
493RD BOMB GROUP	860TH BOMB SQDN	861ST BOMB SQDN	862ND BOMB SQDN	863RD BOMB SQDN

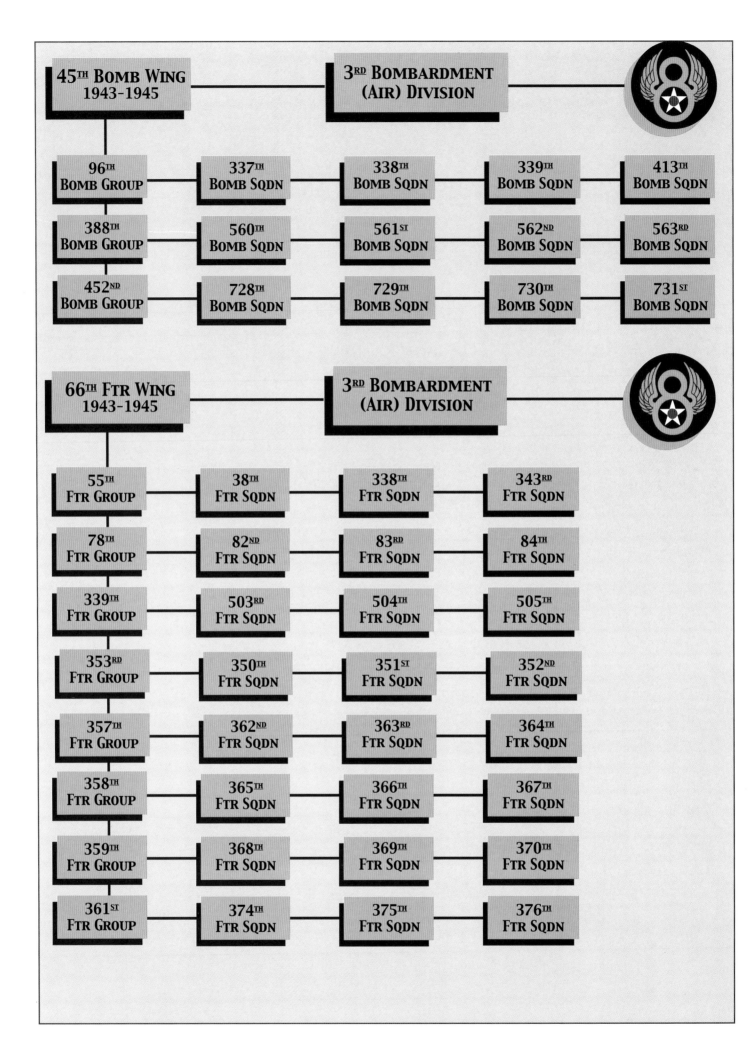

45TH BOMB WING 1943-1945 — **3RD BOMBARDMENT (AIR) DIVISION**

96TH BOMB GROUP	337TH BOMB SQDN	338TH BOMB SQDN	339TH BOMB SQDN	413TH BOMB SQDN
388TH BOMB GROUP	560TH BOMB SQDN	561ST BOMB SQDN	562ND BOMB SQDN	563RD BOMB SQDN
452ND BOMB GROUP	728TH BOMB SQDN	729TH BOMB SQDN	730TH BOMB SQDN	731ST BOMB SQDN

66TH FTR WING 1943-1945 — **3RD BOMBARDMENT (AIR) DIVISION**

55TH FTR GROUP	38TH FTR SQDN	338TH FTR SQDN	343RD FTR SQDN
78TH FTR GROUP	82ND FTR SQDN	83RD FTR SQDN	84TH FTR SQDN
339TH FTR GROUP	503RD FTR SQDN	504TH FTR SQDN	505TH FTR SQDN
353RD FTR GROUP	350TH FTR SQDN	351ST FTR SQDN	352ND FTR SQDN
357TH FTR GROUP	362ND FTR SQDN	363RD FTR SQDN	364TH FTR SQDN
358TH FTR GROUP	365TH FTR SQDN	366TH FTR SQDN	367TH FTR SQDN
359TH FTR GROUP	368TH FTR SQDN	369TH FTR SQDN	370TH FTR SQDN
361ST FTR GROUP	374TH FTR SQDN	375TH FTR SQDN	376TH FTR SQDN

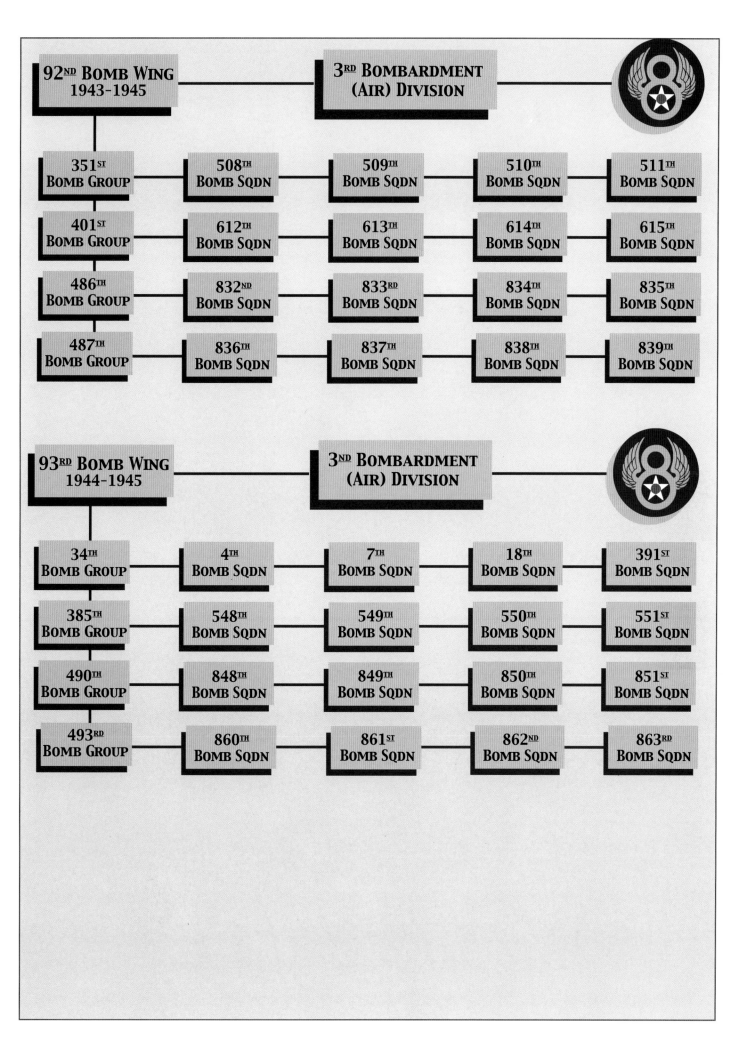

92ND BOMB WING
1943-1945

3RD BOMBARDMENT (AIR) DIVISION

351ST BOMB GROUP	508TH BOMB SQDN	509TH BOMB SQDN	510TH BOMB SQDN	511TH BOMB SQDN
401ST BOMB GROUP	612TH BOMB SQDN	613TH BOMB SQDN	614TH BOMB SQDN	615TH BOMB SQDN
486TH BOMB GROUP	832ND BOMB SQDN	833RD BOMB SQDN	834TH BOMB SQDN	835TH BOMB SQDN
487TH BOMB GROUP	836TH BOMB SQDN	837TH BOMB SQDN	838TH BOMB SQDN	839TH BOMB SQDN

93RD BOMB WING
1944-1945

3ND BOMBARDMENT (AIR) DIVISION

34TH BOMB GROUP	4TH BOMB SQDN	7TH BOMB SQDN	18TH BOMB SQDN	391ST BOMB SQDN
385TH BOMB GROUP	548TH BOMB SQDN	549TH BOMB SQDN	550TH BOMB SQDN	551ST BOMB SQDN
490TH BOMB GROUP	848TH BOMB SQDN	849TH BOMB SQDN	850TH BOMB SQDN	851ST BOMB SQDN
493RD BOMB GROUP	860TH BOMB SQDN	861ST BOMB SQDN	862ND BOMB SQDN	863RD BOMB SQDN

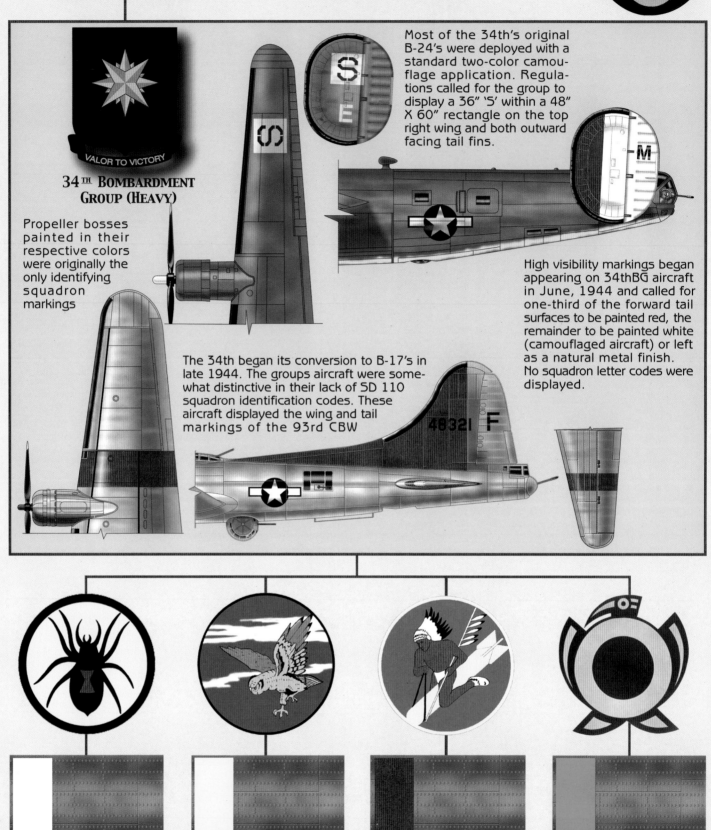

VALOR TO VICTORY

34TH **BOMBARDMENT GROUP (HEAVY)**

Propeller bosses painted in their respective colors were originally the only identifying squadron markings

Most of the 34th's original B-24's were deployed with a standard two-color camouflage application. Regulations called for the group to display a 36" 'S' within a 48" X 60" rectangle on the top right wing and both outward facing tail fins.

The 34th began its conversion to B-17's in late 1944. The groups aircraft were somewhat distinctive in their lack of SD 110 squadron identification codes. These aircraft displayed the wing and tail markings of the 93rd CBW

High visibility markings began appearing on 34thBG aircraft in June, 1944 and called for one-third of the forward tail surfaces to be painted red, the remainder to be painted white (camouflaged aircraft) or left as a natural metal finish. No squadron letter codes were displayed.

48321 F

4TH **BMB SQDN**

7TH **BMB SQDN**

18TH **BMB SQDN**

391ST **BMB SQDN**

•34TH BOMBARDMENT GROUP (HEAVY)•
'VALOR TO VICTORY'
STATION NO.156
MENDLESHAM A/F, SUFFOLK
•CAMPAIGNS•
ANTISUBMARINE, AMERICAN THEATER
AIR OFFENSIVE-EUROPE • NORMANDY
NORTHERN FRANCE • RHINELAND
ARDENNES-ALSACE • CENTRAL EUROPE
•ASSIGNED EIGHTH AIR FORCE•
APRIL, 1944-JULY, 1945

For some reason the 34th Bomb Group elected not to display the assigned SD110 squadron codes on its aircraft. This policy was adopted upon the groups initial deployment in England with its original allocation of B-24 Liberators and would continue to be adhered to even after the groups transition to B-17's. It was not until after the end of hostilities in Europe that the 34thBG was required to apply standard unit identification markings as part of the Army's 'anti-buzzing' efforts.

Although the squadron insignia depicted on the facing page was the authorized version for the 4th Bomb Squadron, the above image was the popular variation displayed by this unit during WWII. At the time of this writing many 34th BG veterans associations still recognize this insignia as representing the 4th BS.

The 34thBG did adopt for use on their B-17's, the application in squadron colors of a 24" nose stripe similar to that depicted in the illustration below. The last three digits of the aircraft serial number was often, but not always, painted in 10"-12" black letters on the lower area of the color band just below the cheek guns.

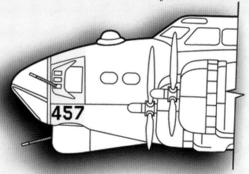

A rectangular tactical identification configuration similar to those below were a further adaptation of the 34thBG late in the war. These consisted of three 12" black stripes, approximately 36" in height, interspaced between three 12" stripes of each squadrons respective color. These markings were sometimes applied in a checkerboard pattern incorporating the same color schemes. When painted on the group's aircraft they were positioned just below the rear gunners station. It appears that the application of these patterns was not obligatory and not all ships were so adorned. Some gunners reportedly felt that such markings served little purpose other than to provide enemy pilots with a convenient aiming point on their station when attacking from the rear.

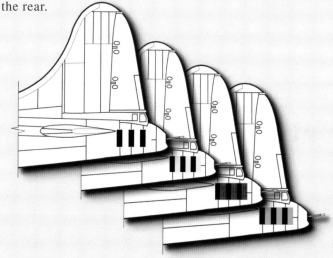

This war time photo of the 'Flying Dutchman' s/n 43-38286 belonging to the 7th Bomb Squadron clearly shows the lack of customary unit tactical markings among 34thBG aircraft.

14TH COMBAT BOMBARDMENT WING (H)

2ND BOMBARDMENT (AIR) DIVISION

AGGRESSOR BEWARE

44TH BOMBARDMENT GROUP (HEAVY)

The 'circle A' configuration began to appear on 44thBG aircraft in the summer of 1943, shortly after return of detachments temporarily assigned to duty in North Africa.

The white disc located on the outside face of both fins varied in size from between 69" to 72" in diameter. The 48" high letter 'A' was typically 48" to 52" in height.

Allied I.D. marker displayed on tails of group B-24's that served temporarily in N. Africa.

Propeller bosses were painted in squadron colors beginning in early 1944

The new high-visiability markings first began to appear in May, 1944. When applying these markings to camouflaged aircraft the entire outer tail surface was often painted white over which the black band was applied.

The 44thBG adopted the following system of aircraft call-letters in November, 1944;

66thBS----	A+ THRU Z+
67thBS----	A THRU Z
68thBS----	A THRU Z
506thBS--	Ā THRU Z

The letter **'I'** was never known to have been used by the 68th or 506th Bomb Squadrons.

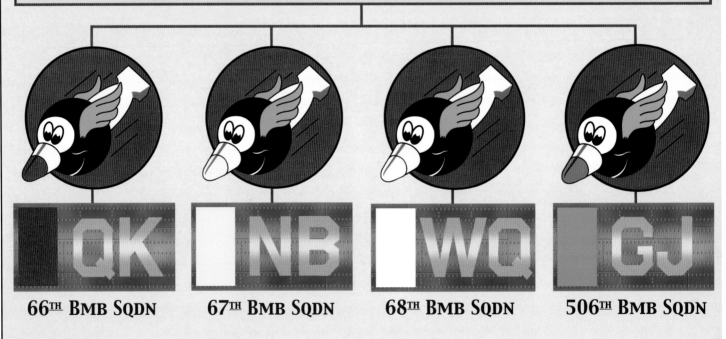

66TH BMB SQDN

67TH BMB SQDN

68TH BMB SQDN

506TH BMB SQDN

•44TH BOMBARDMENT GROUP (HEAVY)•
THE 'FLYING EIGHT BALLS'
STATION NO.115
SHIPDHAM A/F-NORFOLK
•CAMPAIGNS•
ANTISUBMARINE, AMERICAN THEATER
AIR COMBAT, EAME THEATER
AIR OFFENSIVE-EUROPE • SICILY
NAPLES-FOGGIA • NORMANDY
NORTHERN FRANCE • RHINELAND
ARDENNES-ALSACE • CENTRAL EUROPE
•ASSIGNED EIGHTH AF•
OCTOBER, 1942-JUNE, 1945

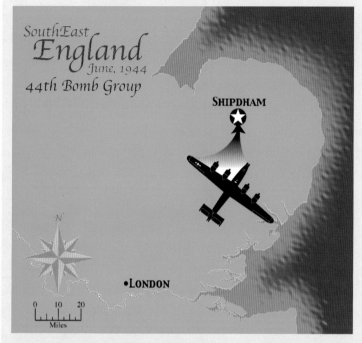

These three aircraft belonging to the 66th Bomb Group show the application of the high-visibility markings to natural metal surfaces. In addition to the partially obscured code letters on the fuselage, the absence of a bar or plus sign adjacent to the tail fin call-letter helps identify the aircraft in the foreground as belonging to the 68th Bomb Squadron.

The application of the Flying Eight Ball insignia to aircraft was a common practice in all squadrons of the 44th Bomb Group. This photo depicts the 44 BG's war weary assembly ship with the group insignia painted on the left side of the aircraft's nose. Although very faint in this image, the individual squadron color rings are nevertheless somewhat discernible.

Although the insignia depicted on the facing page was the 'semiofficial' unit marker for the 44thBG (finally approved in 1951), the Flying Eight Ball image is the symbol that best represents this unit during the course of World War II. Being an unofficial unit emblem there were several variations to this design in both line and color configuration. These variants however were minimal and this image was never mistaken as representing anything other than the 44th Bombardment Group.

The Group insignia is identified by the application of all four squadron colors within the confines of the drawings 'nose' regardless of configuration. As a means of individual identification, each squadron applied its specific color code to this same area as can be seen on the preceding page.

The 44th's 'semiofficial' group insignia was not the only casualty of war. The cartoon depicted above was designed by Disney Studios for the 67th Bomb Squadron prior to the 44thBG's deployment overseas, and was officially approved by the Army in July, 1943. For whatever reasons, this image was shelved when the unit shipped out for England, a not uncommon occurrence and many other stateside/peacetime generated insignia were to share a similar fate.

1ST COMBAT BOMBARDMENT WING (H)

1ST BOMBARDMENT (AIR) DIVISION

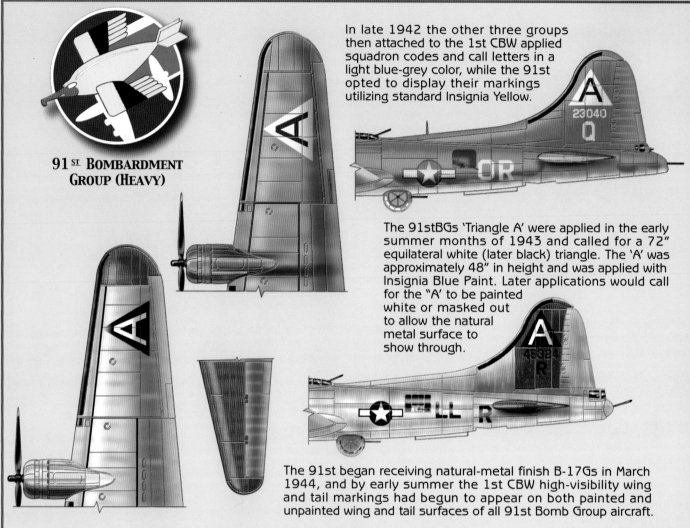

91ST BOMBARDMENT GROUP (HEAVY)

In late 1942 the other three groups then attached to the 1st CBW applied squadron codes and call letters in a light blue-grey color, while the 91st opted to display their markings utilizing standard Insignia Yellow.

The 91stBGs 'Triangle A' were applied in the early summer months of 1943 and called for a 72" equilateral white (later black) triangle. The 'A' was approximately 48" in height and was applied with Insignia Blue Paint. Later applications would call for the "A" to be painted white or masked out to allow the natural metal surface to show through.

The 91st began receiving natural-metal finish B-17Gs in March 1944, and by early summer the 1st CBW high-visibility wing and tail markings had begun to appear on both painted and unpainted wing and tail surfaces of all 91st Bomb Group aircraft.

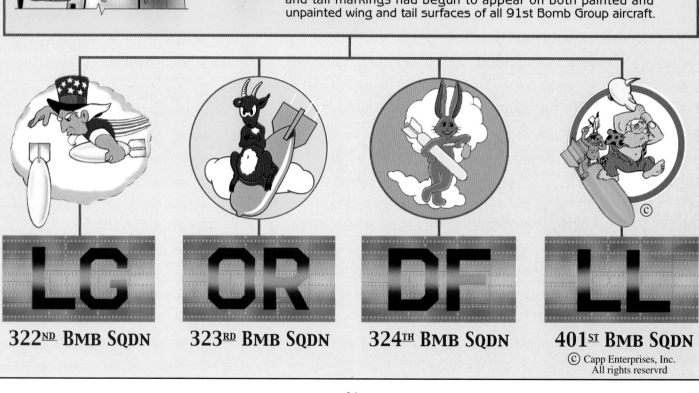

LG
322ND BMB SQDN

OR
323RD BMB SQDN

DF
324TH BMB SQDN

LL
401ST BMB SQDN

•91ˢᵀ Bombardment Group (Heavy)•
'The Ragged Irregulars'
•Station No.121•
Bassingbourn A/F • Cambridgeshire
•Campaigns•
Air Offensive-Europe • Normandy
Northern France • Rhineland
Ardennes-Alsace • Central Europe
•Assigned Eighth Air Force•
September, 1942-June, 1945

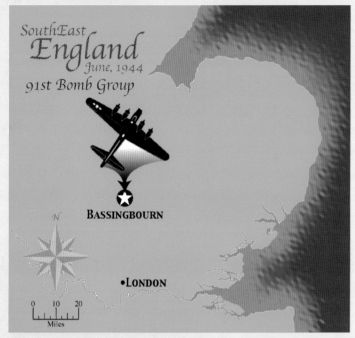

Upon its deployment to England the 91stBomb Group was first equipped with two color camouflaged B-17Fs. Some, but not all of these would received a further treatment of Medium Green paint applied to the Olive Drab upper surface in a random variegate pattern. This 'field application' was a crude means of providing additional camouflaging protection. The 91stBG saw its first action in November 1942 and within a month the newly assigned squadron codes and call letters began to appear on all group aircraft. The photo below depicts a typical 91stBG marking configuration. The blue and white national insignia would indicate a post September 1943 time frame for this particular photograph.

To the right can be seen the distinctive high visibility tail markings of the 1stCBW that began to appear on 91st BG aircraft in the early summer of 1944. Note that the Insignia Blue on white 'Triangle A' configuration has been replaced with a white-on-black application. On painted aircraft the 'A' was applied with Insignia Yellow over a black triangle and this remained the standard until wars end.

The photo below abounds with clues which, when taken as a whole, provides the researcher with enough facts to trace this aircrafts' deployment history. (A) The 'Triangle A' on the tail denotes this as belonging to the 91st Bomb Group. (B) The national insignia displayed on this ship was replaced by the familiar red outlined 'star and bars' pattern in June, 1943. (C) Squadron markings were first applied to 91st Bomb Group aircraft in December, 1942. These particular markings tell us that this B-17 was assigned to the 323rd Bomb Squadron with the call-letter 'P'. (D) Even though the first digits of the aircraft serial number are partially obscured or missing in this photo, the remaining four digits are legible and thus helpful in further research. (E) Judging by the open in-line waist gun positions this would appear to be an 'F' series B-17. It should be noted however, that some of the early 'G' series were produced with this configuration prior to converting to a staggered gun window pattern.

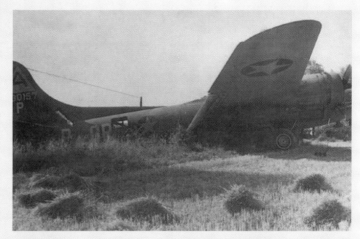

In the above photo, application of the Insignia Blue 'A' on a white triangle can be clearly seen on the aircrafts top right wing surface.

35

92ND BOMBARDMENT GROUP (HEAVY)

HIGHER·STRONGER·FASTER

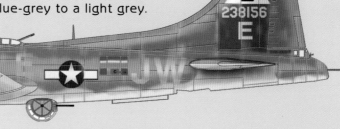

SD110 codes first began to appear on 92nd BG aircraft in December, 1942. 36" high squadron letters were applied in colors ranging from a blue-grey to a light grey.

The 'Triangle B' device was introduced to 92nd BG ships in June, 1943. Specifications called for a 60" pattern and a 72" pattern applied to the tail and top right wing respectively. Although these specifications called for the letter in Insignia Blue, black was a common substitute.

The use of color as a means of identification was limited and sporadic within the 92nd. The one exception was the 327th Bomb Squadron which, in the summer of 1944, adopted the practice of painting all its' aircrafts propeller bosses blue.

The addition of a 48" wide red band to all 92nd BG tail sections was implemented in August, 1944.

The regulation governing placement of the call-letter and squadron code was modified in April, 1943.

NV

JW

UX

PY

325TH BMB SQDN

326TH BMB SQDN

327TH BMB SQDN

407TH BMB SQDN

•92ND BOMBARDMENT GROUP (HEAVY)•
'HIGHER•STRONGER•FASTER'
•STATION NO.102•
ALCONBURY A/F • HUNTINGDONSHIRE
•CAMPAIGNS•
ANTISUBMARINE, AMERICAN THEATER
AIR OFFENSIVE-EUROPE • NORMANDY
NORTHERN FRANCE • RHINELAND
ARDENNES-ALSACE • CENTRAL EUROPE
•ASSIGNED EIGHTH AF•
AUGUST, 1942-JULY, 1945

The aerial shot below gives the researcher a good view of the groups second generation 'Triangle B' in its' standard location outboard the top right wing surface. Beginning in early 1944 the group marker began to be applied to the *underside* of their aircrafts' left wing as well. This application was not unique to the 92nd but was in fact a policy adapted by the 40th CBW for all units under its' command.

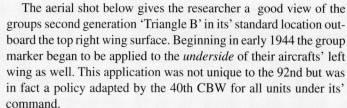

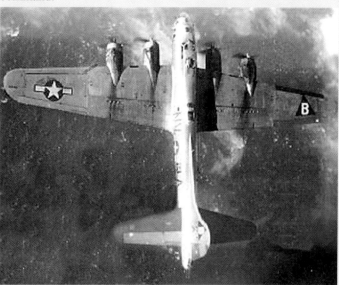

Below is a good tail shot of a transition period 92nd BG aircraft. Note that this example has adopted the revised squadron code/ call-letter configuration on the fuselage and displays the groups triangle marker, but lacks the application of a horizontal red stripe to the rear horizontal stabilizer. Given what is known about these markings, the date of this photo can probably be safely estimated as falling somewhere between June 1943 and August 1944.

With the exception of a few limited tactical missions during the months of September and October 1942, the 92nd Bomb Groups combat operations did not get under way in full scale until May, 1943. As with all of the first Eighth AF bombardment groups to deploy in England, aircraft markings were sparce, consisting of little more than the national insignia applied to wing and fuselage surfaces and the aircrafts identification number affixed to the tail.

Left: A couple of 92nd Bomb Group ground crew personnel pose for a snapshot in front of two B-17Fs, obviously assigned to the 325th Bomb Squadron.

The photo below is an excellent example of a late war 92nd BG tactical marking configuration.

93RD BOMBARDMENT GROUP (HEAVY)

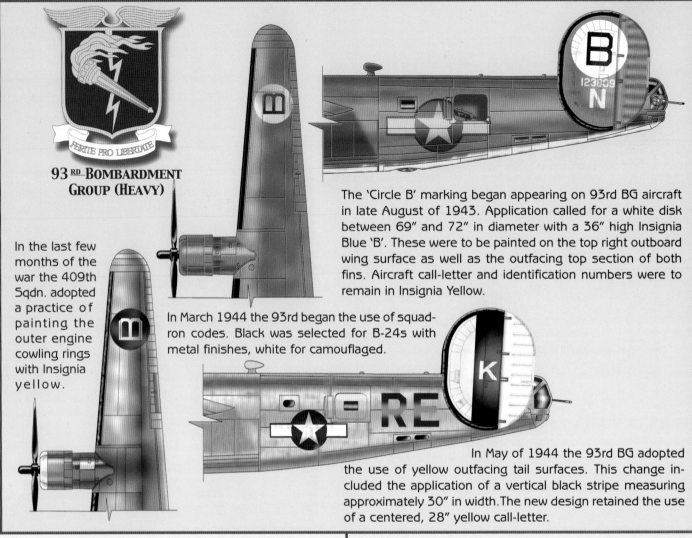

In the last few months of the war the 409th Sqdn. adopted a practice of painting the outer engine cowling rings with Insignia yellow.

The 'Circle B' marking began appearing on 93rd BG aircraft in late August of 1943. Application called for a white disk between 69" and 72" in diameter with a 36" high Insignia Blue 'B'. These were to be painted on the top right outboard wing surface as well as the outfacing top section of both fins. Aircraft call-letter and identification numbers were to remain in Insignia Yellow.

In March 1944 the 93rd began the use of squadron codes. Black was selected for B-24s with metal finishes, white for camouflaged.

In May of 1944 the 93rd BG adopted the use of yellow outfacing tail surfaces. This change included the application of a vertical black stripe measuring approximately 30" in width. The new design retained the use of a centered, 28" yellow call-letter.

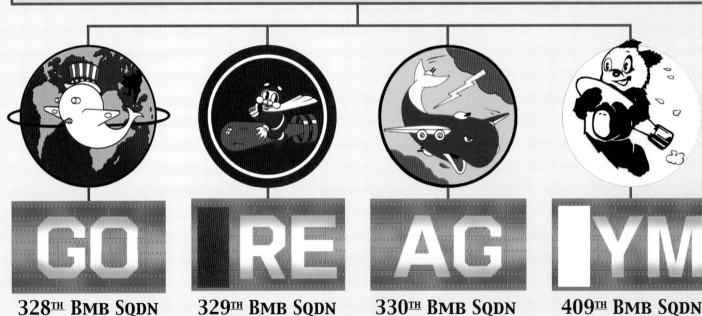

GO	RE	AG	YM
328TH BMB SQDN	329TH BMB SQDN	330TH BMB SQDN	409TH BMB SQDN

•93RD BOMBARDMENT GROUP (HEAVY)•
'THE TRAVELLING CIRCUS'
•STATION NO.104•
HARDWICK AF-NORFOLK COUNTY
•CAMPAIGNS•
ANTISUBMARINE, AMERICAN THEATER
AIR COMBAT, EAME THEATER
EGYPT-LIBYA • TUNISIA
SICILY • NAPLES-FOGGIA
AIR OFFENSIVE-EUROPE • NORMANDY
NORTHERN FRANCE • RHINELAND
ARDENNES-ALSACE • CENTRAL EUROPE
•ASSIGNED EIGHTH AF•
SEPTEMBER, 1942-MAY, 1945

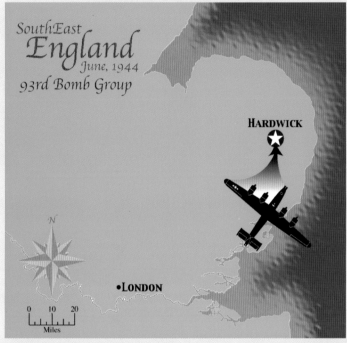

The 93rd was the first American B-24 unit to be deployed to England and entered combat on October 9 1942, shortly after its arrival. In November three of the groups four squadrons, the 328th, 330th and 409th, were detached TDY to North Africa for combat duty with the Twelfth and later the Ninth AF. These squadrons returned to England in late February, 1943, but the Group would be detached for temporary duty with the Ninth AF on two more occasions. It was these very assignments that earned the group its nickname;
'The Traveling Circus'.

An interesting shot from a position on top of the left wing looking down over the number two engine cowling. This angle affords a good view of the 409th Bomb Squadrons 'Panda' insignia affixed just below the navigators window. The 409th seemingly took a great deal of pride in this symbol as it pops-up numerous times in photo records of the 93rd Bomb Group. The other three squadrons apparently did not share this affinity for their respective insignia as these symbols are rarely seen applied to aircraft in war time photographs. Some of the 330th BGs aircraft did, however adopt a 'whale face' configuration reflective of the squadrons official insignia. These designs were painted on the noses of several of the units B-24s using black and white paint.

This unexpected visit at Watton A/F by a B-24D of the 93rdBG took place in November, 1943. Of special interest is the 409th Squadrons insignia painted on the nose and the national insignia still carries the red outline which had been officially replaced with Insignia Blue two months earlier.

Prior to the adaptation of the 'Circle B' devise, B-24s of the 93rd displayed little more on their fins than a call-letter and the aircrafts' individual I.D. number applied with Insignia Yellow. Those aircraft returning from deployment in North Africa carried a tri-color 18X24 inch RAF fin flash like that depicted in the illustration to the left. Although not authorized for display by American bombers based in Great Britain, these devises nevertheless remained on 93rd BG B-24s until finally removed in the late summer of 1943.

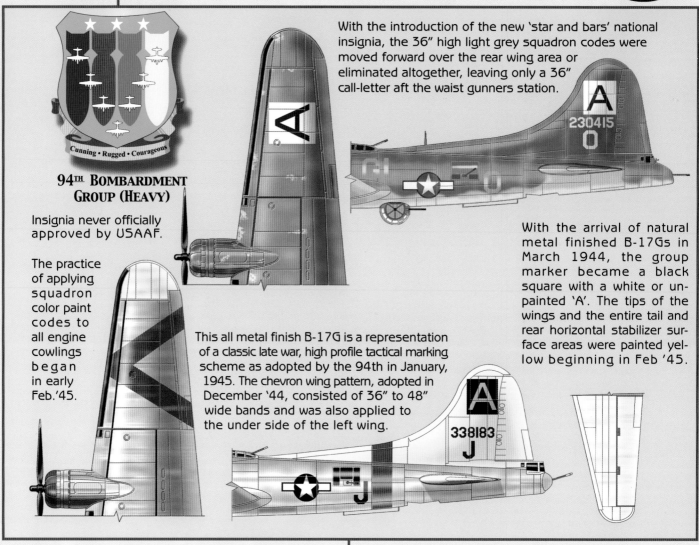

94TH BOMBARDMENT GROUP (HEAVY)

Cunning · Rugged · Courageous

Insignia never officially approved by USAAF.

The practice of applying squadron color paint codes to all engine cowlings began in early Feb.'45.

With the introduction of the new 'star and bars' national insignia, the 36" high light grey squadron codes were moved forward over the rear wing area or eliminated altogether, leaving only a 36" call-letter aft the waist gunners station.

This all metal finish B-17G is a representation of a classic late war, high profile tactical marking scheme as adopted by the 94th in January, 1945. The chevron wing pattern, adopted in December '44, consisted of 36" to 48" wide bands and was also applied to the under side of the left wing.

With the arrival of natural metal finished B-17Gs in March 1944, the group marker became a black square with a white or unpainted 'A'. The tips of the wings and the entire tail and rear horizontal stabilizer surface areas were painted yellow beginning in Feb '45.

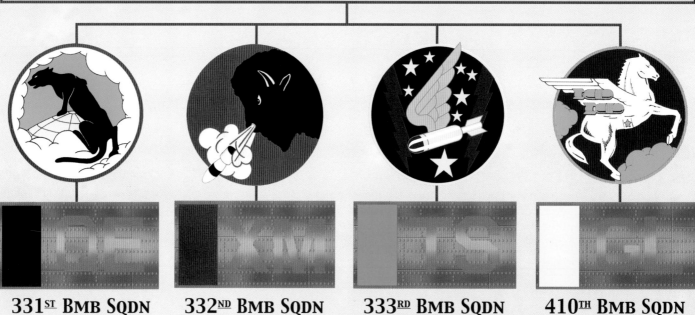

331ST BMB SQDN

332ND BMB SQDN

333RD BMB SQDN

410TH BMB SQDN

•94TH BOMBARDMENT GROUP (HEAVY)•
'CUNNING•RUGGED•COURAGEOUS'
•STATION NO.468•
BURY ST EDMUNDS AF • SUFFOLK COUNTY
•CAMPAIGNS•
AIR OFFENSIVE-EUROPE • NORMANDY
NORTHERN FRANCE • RHINELAND
ARDENNES-ALSACE • CENTRAL EUROPE
•ASSIGNED EIGHTH AF•
MAY, 1943-JULY, 1945

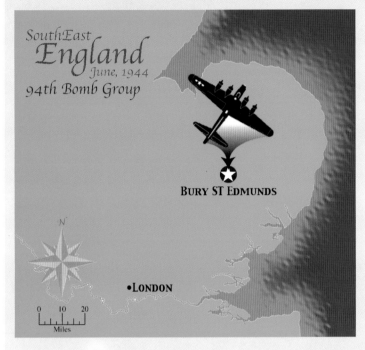

The 94th entered combat within a month of its arrival in England. The groups inventory of B-17Fs were a standard Olive Drab, dark with a Neutral Grey applied to the under surfaces. Squadron codes were applied soon after the group settled in at its new base.

The 94th Bomb Groups marker was adopted at about the same time and called for a 48"X60" white rectangle which was to include a 36" high Insignia Blue letter 'A', in practice however, this rectangular configuration would sometimes more closely resemble a square. Within a few months the design specifications were modified to allow for 48"X48" application to the tail assembly, the spec's for the letter remained the same.

This formation shot of B-17Fs reveals little initial information for the researcher other than the obvious tail marker of the 94th Bomb Group. With this as a starting point however, we have the lead aircrafts' serial number and call-letter and a little research into the groups history and the ship in the foreground is identified as 'Virgins Delight' belonging to the 333rd Bomb Squadron.

This 3/4 aft view of B-17F 'Northern Queen' provides a fairly good detail shot of a 94th BG marker configuration. Of special note here is the difference in the grey values on the tail section. At first glance this ship could be mistaken as belonging to the 1st Combat Bomb Wing due to the darker center tail area which, in a black and white photo, might be misconstrued as an application of red paint, the tactical markings of the 91st, 381st and 398th Bomb Sqdns.

The bottom illustration and photograph are submitted as further evidence that there are no absolutes when it comes to the study of AAF insignia and markings during World War Two. The squadron insignia featured on the previous page is one representation of the emblem for the 333rd Bomb Squadron during the war, and we happen to have this photo to verify its existence and use. On the other hand we have the image below which appears to have been an earlier insignia. In neither one of these cases however were the designs ever officially approved by the 'proper authority', so the problem becomes one of deciding which of the two should be included in the text as representing the 333rd BG. The fact is that they both represent the 333rd, only at different times. Thus both are presented herein and the reader is free to make a subjective evaluation as to which is the better of the two.

It should be mentioned that the 94th BG insignia depicted on the facing page was never officially approved and several variations are known to exist, this being one of the more elaborate designs.

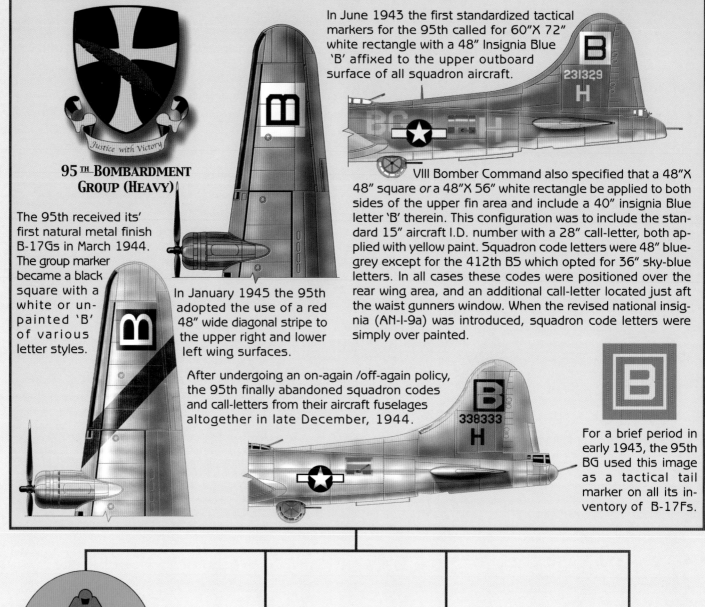

95TH BOMBARDMENT GROUP (HEAVY)

In June 1943 the first standardized tactical markers for the 95th called for 60"X 72" white rectangle with a 48" Insignia Blue 'B' affixed to the upper outboard surface of all squadron aircraft.

The 95th received its' first natural metal finish B-17Gs in March 1944. The group marker became a black square with a white or un-painted 'B' of various letter styles.

In January 1945 the 95th adopted the use of a red 48" wide diagonal stripe to the upper right and lower left wing surfaces.

After undergoing an on-again /off-again policy, the 95th finally abandoned squadron codes and call-letters from their aircraft fuselages altogether in late December, 1944.

VIII Bomber Command also specified that a 48"X 48" square *or* a 48"X 56" white rectangle be applied to both sides of the upper fin area and include a 40" insignia Blue letter 'B' therein. This configuration was to include the standard 15" aircraft I.D. number with a 28" call-letter, both applied with yellow paint. Squadron code letters were 48" blue-grey except for the 412th BS which opted for 36" sky-blue letters. In all cases these codes were positioned over the rear wing area, and an additional call-letter located just aft the waist gunners window. When the revised national insignia (AN-I-9a) was introduced, squadron code letters were simply over painted.

For a brief period in early 1943, the 95th BG used this image as a tactical tail marker on all its inventory of B-17Fs.

334TH BMB SQDN

335TH BMB SQDN

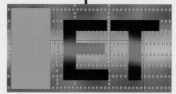

336TH BMB SQDN

412TH BMB SQDN

•95TH BOMBARDMENT GROUP (HEAVY)•
'JUSTICE WITH VICTORY'
STATION NO.119
HORHAM A/F-SUFFOLK
•CAMPAIGNS•
AIR OFFENSIVE-EUROPE • NORMANDY
NORTHERN FRANCE • RHINELAND
ARDENNES-ALSACE • CENTRAL EUROPE
•ASSIGNED EIGHTH AF•
MAY, 1943-JUNE, 1945

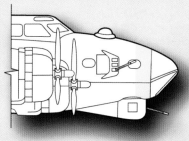

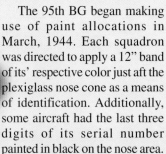

The 95th BG began making use of paint allocations in March, 1944. Each squadron was directed to apply a 12" band of its' respective color just aft the plexiglass nose cone as a means of identification. Additionally, some aircraft had the last three digits of its serial number painted in black on the nose area.

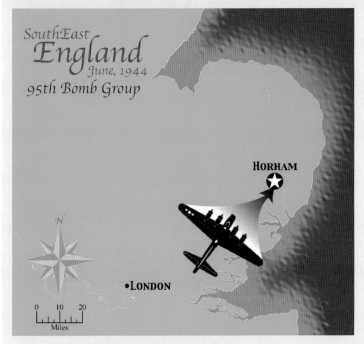

The similar application of a band of squadron color just below the tail gunners station was encouraged but not a group requirement. In January 1945, the 95th began applying a 48" wide band of red paint to the vertical stabilizers on all its aircraft. This color configuration measured approximately 48" in width and conformed to the angle of the fins trailing edge, starting at the top of the fin and terminating at the shelf area of the empennage.

The 95th Bomb Group wasted no time after its deployment in England, jumping into combat within weeks of setting up shop first at Framlingham then Horham Air Fields. Upon its arrival in the British Isles the 95th employed a unique method of squadron identification, a hypothetical example of which is presented below;

Each vertical 12" long bar represented one of the four squadrons comprising the 95th BG, thus;

one stripe.........334th Bomb Squadron
two stripes.......335th Bomb Squadron
three stripes.....336th Bomb Squadron
four stripes......412th Bomb Squadron

The group did not long retain this configuration once it reached England, but this particular use of linear patterns constituted a rather unique early solution to the problem of individual squadron identification, and as such warranted inclusion within this text.

The two photographs above show the application of the 95th BG tactical marker to the upper right wing surface. Additionally, although barely discernible in this image, the diagonal red wing stripe denoting the 95th Bomb Group can nevertheless be detected in the lower photo.

To the left is an excellent 'on-the-job' photo giving a good glimpse of the original tactical tail markings of a 95th bomber. This ship carries the newer Type 3 or 4 national insignia with what appears to be a yellow or white contour outline.

45ᵀᴴ COMBAT BOMBARDMENT WING (H)

3ᴿᴰ BOMBARDMENT (AIR) DIVISION

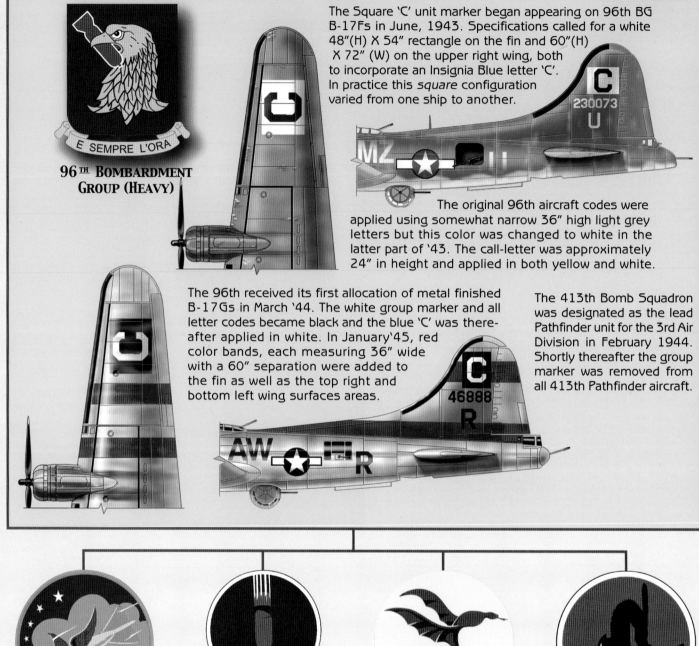

96ᵀᴴ BOMBARDMENT GROUP (HEAVY)

E SEMPRE L'ORA

The Square 'C' unit marker began appearing on 96th BG B-17Fs in June, 1943. Specifications called for a white 48"(H) X 54" rectangle on the fin and 60"(H) X 72" (W) on the upper right wing, both to incorporate an Insignia Blue letter 'C'. In practice this *square* configuration varied from one ship to another.

The original 96th aircraft codes were applied using somewhat narrow 36" high light grey letters but this color was changed to white in the latter part of '43. The call-letter was approximately 24" in height and applied in both yellow and white.

The 96th received its first allocation of metal finished B-17Gs in March '44. The white group marker and all letter codes became black and the blue 'C' was there-after applied in white. In January'45, red color bands, each measuring 36" wide with a 60" separation were added to the fin as well as the top right and bottom left wing surfaces areas.

The 413th Bomb Squadron was designated as the lead Pathfinder unit for the 3rd Air Division in February 1944. Shortly thereafter the group marker was removed from all 413th Pathfinder aircraft.

337ᵀᴴ BMB SQDN

338ᵀᴴ BMB SQDN

339ᵀᴴ BMB SQDN

413ᵀᴴ BMB SQDN

•96TH BOMBARDMENT GROUP (HEAVY)•
'IT IS ALWAYS THE HOUR'
•STATION NO.138•
SNETTERTON HEATH A/F-NORFOLK
•CAMPAIGNS•
AIR OFFENSIVE-EUROPE • NORMANDY
NORTHERN FRANCE • RHINELAND
ARDENNES-ALSACE • CENTRAL EUROPE
•ASSIGNED EIGHTH AF•
MAY,1943-JULY,1945

These two battle damage photos provide a fairly good close-up look of the application of an early 96th Bomb Group Tactical tail marking and the standard placement of the squadron code and aircraft call-letter to the fuselage. Note that the serial numbers on the tail have not been filled in and stencil lines are still evident.

96th Bomb Group aircraft began receiving group recognition markings soon after its deployment to England. With the later introduction of staggered waist gun stations, the arrangement of squadron codes to the fuselage became a rather random affair. On one ship the squadron code and call-letter might be grouped together while another more or less adhered to specifications. Placement of these codes often resembled something more akin to a game of 'pin-the-tail-on-the-donkey' than adherence to established guidelines.

The bottom left photograph shows the proper size and placement of a first pattern blue-on-white 96th BG tactical wing marker.

When studying a large number of period photos relating to the 96th, a variety of shapes pertaining to this particular image becomes apparent. Applications varied from an true square to rectangular configurations, some applied vertically, others horizontally.

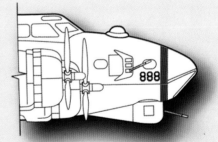

In July 1944 the 96th issued color codes to all squadrons except the 413th, due to its low profile status as a Pathfinder unit. These codes manifested themselves as 6" paint bands applied just aft the ships nose cone. Use of these color bands became infrequent by January 1945. It was during this period that the 96th began the sporadic painting of the last three serial number digits to the aircraft's nose. This treatment was not rigidly adhered to however, and not all squadron B-17s were so marked.

1ST COMBAT BOMBARDMENT WING (H)

1ST BOMBARDMENT (AIR) DIVISION

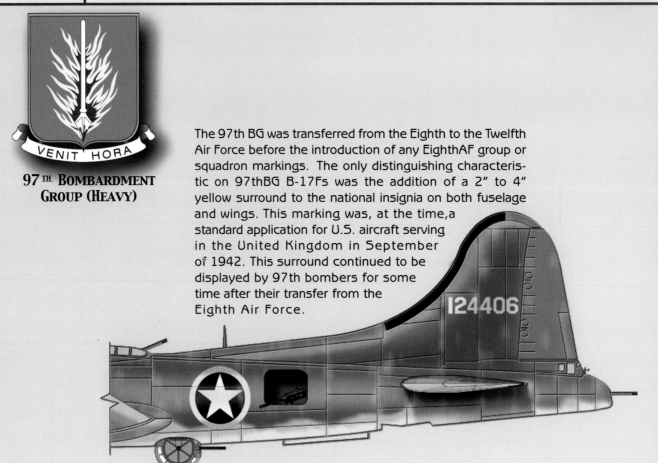

VENIT HORA

97TH BOMBARDMENT GROUP (HEAVY)

The 97th BG was transferred from the Eighth to the Twelfth Air Force before the introduction of any EighthAF group or squadron markings. The only distinguishing characteristic on 97thBG B-17Fs was the addition of a 2" to 4" yellow surround to the national insignia on both fuselage and wings. This marking was, at the time, a standard application for U.S. aircraft serving in the United Kingdom in September of 1942. This surround continued to be displayed by 97th bombers for some time after their transfer from the Eighth Air Force.

124406

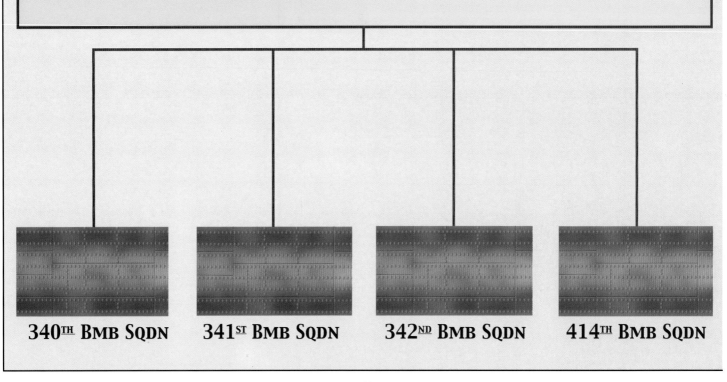

| 340TH BMB SQDN | 341ST BMB SQDN | 342ND BMB SQDN | 414TH BMB SQDN |

•97th Bombardment Group (Heavy)•
'The Hour Has Come'
•Station No.110 & 106•
Polebrook A/F & Grafton-Underwood A/F
•Campaigns•
Antisubmarine, American Theater
Air Combat, EAME Theater
Air Offensive-Europe • Tunisia
Sicily•Naples-Foggia • Anzio • Normandy
Northern France • Southern France
North Apennines • Rhineland
Central Europe • Po Valley
•Assigned Eighth AF•
June, 1942-November, 1942

Even though their assignment to the Eighth Air Force was for a brief period, the 97th Bomb Group nevertheless flew a total of sixteen combat missions while so assigned, and in spite of the fact that this unit was totally devoid of individual group/squadron markings, it was considered important that it be included in this work. A quick review of the 97th Bomb Groups campaign credits (as listed above) attests to the fact that this units combat involvement did not end with its' transfer from the Eighth Air Force. The 97th went on to serve with distinction with the Twelfth and later the Fifteenth Air Forces, but this period of the groups history has been relegated to a subsequent volume.

This insignia was designed by Disney Studios for the 342nd Bombardment Squadron when the 97th Bomb Group was stationed in Florida at either MacDill Field or Sarasota-Bradenton Air Field. Whether or not this insignia was ever displayed by the 342nd once the 97th deployed to England is unknown, but it is nice visual part of the units history, and thus deemed appropriate to be included herein.

13TH COMBAT BOMBARDMENT WING (H)

3RD BOMBARDMENT (AIR) DIVISION

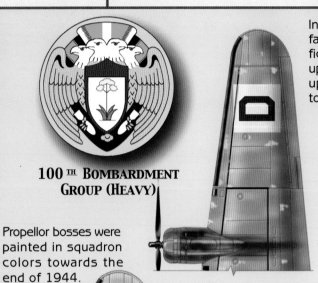

100TH BOMBARDMENT GROUP (HEAVY)

In July '43 the 100th BG adopted the use of the now famous 'Square D' tactical marker. The original specifications called for a 48" White square on the upper tail fin area and a 66" square on the upper right wing surface, both of which to incorporate a 36" Insignia Blue 'D'.

Propellor bosses were painted in squadron colors towards the end of 1944. Similiarly, 12" color bands were applied just aft the nose cones in early '45.

Squadron codes and call-letters were added to the fuselages about a month earlier. These were 36" tall letters applied with bluish-grey paint. Sky Blue was used as a substitute on some later applications presumably due to a shortage of the original specified color. A additional 24" yellow call-letter was affixed to the fin, just below the 15" aircraft identification number.

In March 1944 the 100th received its' first consignment of natural metal finished B-17Gs. Group tactical markings remained much the same as for the units camouflaged aircraft except that the squares were converted to black and the letter therein to white.

A 36" wide diagonal black band began appearing on 100th BG aircraft in early 1945. These devises were affixed to the upper right and lower left outboard wing surface areas.

In February 1945 the 100th further adopted the use of an all black rudder as a means of complying with the directive relating to high visibility markings.

349TH BMB SQDN

350TH BMB SQDN

351ST BMB SQDN

418TH BMB SQDN

•100TH BOMBARDMENT GROUP (HEAVY)•
'THE BLOODY HUNDREDTH'
•STATION NO.139•
THORPE ABBOTTS A/F • NORFOLK
•CAMPAIGNS•
AIR OFFENSIVE-EUROPE • NORMANDY
NORTHERN FRANCE • RHINELAND
ARDENNES-ALSACE • CENTRAL EUROPE
•ASSIGNED EIGHTH AF•
JUNE,1943-JULY,1945

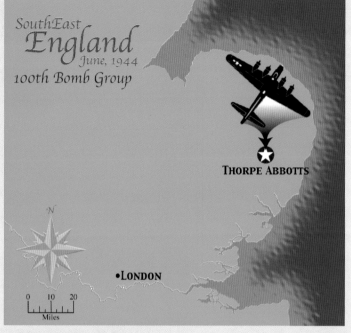

SouthEast
England
June, 1944
100th Bomb Group

THORPE ABBOTTS

•LONDON

0   10   20
Miles

The top salvage yard photo affords us with an unusual but nevertheless informative view of the placement and relative sizes of both the first pattern tail and wing tactical markings.

The next image illustrates the starboard fuselage application on both the aircraft call-letter (aft of the waist gun window) and the squadron code, located on a slightly higher plane, over the rear wing area.

The 100th Bomb Group was late in adopting the high-visibility tactical markings to their aircraft. Originally, the black configuration applied to the fin overlapped the rudder to extend upwards to the tip of the tail itself. This method of identification was short lived however and the application of black paint was soon limited to the confines of the rudder proper.

In some cases involving natural metal finishes, especially on later B-17G series, the letter 'D' was left unpainted with the metal surface showing through the surrounding black square.

Directly below is a good period photo depicting a B-17G of the 418th Bomb Sqdn. Even with the fuselage squadron code markings obscured by the wing, this ships assignment can be established by the red color code markings applied to the propeller bosses and the nose cone area.

The airborne photo at the bottom provides good detail look of the port side application of all tactical markings as applied to a camouflaged 350th Bomb Squadron aircraft.

There is an interesting little story behind the photo to the left, but for the sake of continuity to the theme of this work, we'll have to focus our attention on the 350th BS insignia signboard directly behind the two officers.

49

1ˢᵀ COMBAT BOMBARDMENT WING (H)

1ˢᵀ BOMBARDMENT (AIR) DIVISION

301ˢᵀ BOMBARDMENT GROUP (HEAVY)

The 301st was another group that had no sooner sewn on their Eighth Air Force patches when they found themselves on their way to North Africa with a transfer to the Twelfth Air Force. Their departure preceded the application of any distinguishing 8thAF tactical markings. However brief their stay in England may have been, they did serve with the Eighth and have thus been included in this work in spite of the lack of any Eighth AF tactical adornment.

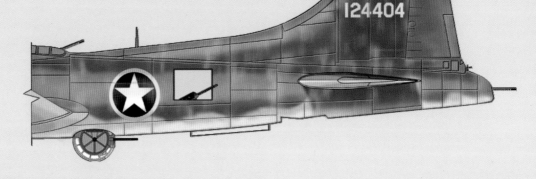

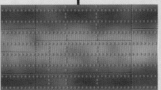

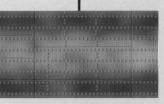

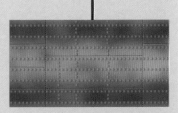

32ᴺᴰ BMB SQDN **352ᴺᴰ BMB SQDN** **353ᴿᴰ BMB SQDN** **419ᵀᴴ BMB SQDN**

•301st Bombardment Group (Heavy)•
'Who Fears ?'
•Station No.139•
Thorpe Abbotts A/F-Norfolk
•Campaigns•
Air Combat, EAME Theater
Air Offensive-Europe • Tunisia
Sicily • Naples-Foggia • Anzio • Rome-Arno
Normandy • Northern France
Southern France • North Apennines
Rhineland • Central Europe • Po Valley
•Assigned Eighth AF•
August, 1942-November, 1942

The group insignia for the 301st was approved by the Army in 1942 while the 32nd Bomb Squadron insignia dates back to 1936. The 352nd, 353rd, and 419th Bomb Squadrons all had insignia approved in 1957, 1959 and 1961 respectively. At the time of this writing however, no information regarding war time insignia for either of these three squadrons was available.

303RD BOMBARDMENT GROUP (HEAVY)

MIGHT IN FLIGHT

The unit crest displayed by the 303rd during WWII differed slightly from the approved version as depicted above.

The 303 first adopted call-letters in October '42. These were 36" high and painted on the tail in yellow or white. Two months later Squadron I.D. codes were assigned and these along with an additional call-letter were affixed as 48" yellow letters to each side of the aircrafts fuselage.

When the new AN-I-9a national insignia was introduced in June '43, the new bars were often simply painted over the existing squadron code. The group marker was adopted in midsummer of '43 and called for a 72" equilateral white triangle incorporating an Insignia Blue letter 'C'. This device was applied to the tail surfaces and the upper right outboard wing tip. These marker colors were changed to a white letter on a black triangle with the first consignment of natural metal finish B-17Gs in March '44.

High visibility markings were officially adopted by the 303rd in August '44. Both tail and wing markers were roughly the same dimensions, however, the wing application lacked the squadron code letter and aircraft identification number.

The letter at the apex of the red triangle denoted each aircrafts squadron assignment, i.e:

1--------358th BS
2--------359th BS
3--------360th BS
4--------427th BS

In some later cases the fuselage codes were eliminated altogether on replacement aircraft.

VN

358TH BMB SQDN

BN

359TH BOMB SQDN

PU

360TH BOMB SQDN

GN

427TH BOMB SQDN

•303RD BOMBARDMENT GROUP (HEAVY)•
'MIGHT IN FLIGHT'
•STATION NO.107•
MOLESWORTH A/F-NORFOLK
•CAMPAIGNS•
AIR OFFENSIVE-EUROPE • NORMANDY
NORTHERN FRANCE • RHINELAND
ARDENNES-ALSACE • CENTRAL EUROPE
•ASSIGNED EIGHTH AF•
SEPTEMBER, 1942-MAY, 1945

Tail shot of 'GI Sheets' of the 427th BS shortly after it crash landed near Soiver-St-Gery, Belgium, 29Jan44. The only unburned section of this aircraft affords a detail view of the application of the 303rd's BG's first pattern marker and tail lettering. Note the unfilled stencil breaks on the aircraft's I.D. numbers.

This image is a more accurate representation of the insignia displayed by the 303rd Bomb Group during the war years.

For the real insignia buffs, this was an early design of the 427th BS just prior to its' Bugs' Bunny look-alike replacement.

Prior to the actual adoption of the 303rd's high-visibility markings, all squadron codes and call-letters were applied with black paint on natural metal finish replacement aircraft.

When the 24" red outline was added to the 303rd's triangle marker, the image size measured approximately ten feet on all linear planes. This necessitated the lowering of the triangle from its' original position to accommodate for the larger overall image size. On some later applications the inner triangle was left unpainted with the 'C' applied in black paint directly to the metal tail surface.

The two photos immediately above and below show the application of the 303rd BG's high-visibility tail markings on both natural metal finished and a camouflaged group B17-Gs. Note that the yellow lettering within the red containment areas does not read all that well in war time b&w photography.

An unusual application of 'nose art' to the starboard fuselage code. The ship was 'Two Beauts' of the 358th Bomb Squadron.

An interesting shot of then Lt. Clark Gable who had just completed his first combat mission aboard 'Eight Ball' on 4May43. As evidenced by the squadron fuselage code, 'Eight Ball' was a B17-F assigned to the 359th Bomb Squadron. Gable was actually assigned to the 508th BS / 351st BG but hitched a ride with the 303rd to begin work on the war time recruitment documentary 'Combat America' that he was producing on behalf of the Army Air Corps.

40TH COMBAT BOMBARDMENT WING (H)

1ST BOMBARDMENT (AIR) DIVISION

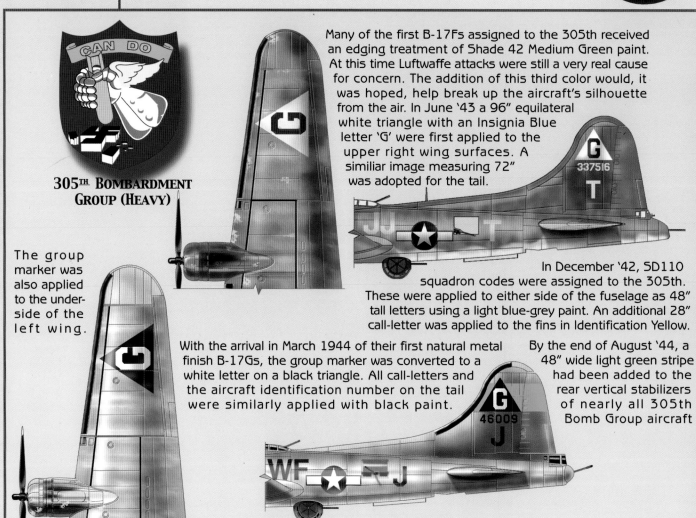

305TH BOMBARDMENT GROUP (HEAVY)

Many of the first B-17Fs assigned to the 305th received an edging treatment of Shade 42 Medium Green paint. At this time Luftwaffe attacks were still a very real cause for concern. The addition of this third color would, it was hoped, help break up the aircraft's silhouette from the air. In June '43 a 96" equilateral white triangle with an Insignia Blue letter 'G' were first applied to the upper right wing surfaces. A similiar image measuring 72" was adopted for the tail.

The group marker was also applied to the underside of the left wing.

In December '42, SD110 squadron codes were assigned to the 305th. These were applied to either side of the fuselage as 48" tall letters using a light blue-grey paint. An additional 28" call-letter was applied to the fins in Identification Yellow.

With the arrival in March 1944 of their first natural metal finish B-17Gs, the group marker was converted to a white letter on a black triangle. All call-letters and the aircraft identification number on the tail were similarly applied with black paint.

By the end of August '44, a 48" wide light green stripe had been added to the rear vertical stabilizers of nearly all 305th Bomb Group aircraft

WF — 364TH BMB SQDN

XK — 365TH BMB SQDN

KY — 366TH BMB SQDN

JJ — 422ND BMB SQDN

•305TH BOMBARDMENT GROUP (HEAVY)•
'CAN DO'
•STATION NO.105•
CHELVESTON A/F–NORTHAMPTONSHIRE
•CAMPAIGNS•
AIR OFFENSIVE-EUROPE • NORMANDY
NORTHERN FRANCE • RHINELAND
ARDENNES-ALSACE • CENTRAL EUROPE
•ASSIGNED EIGHTH AF•
SEPTEMBER, 1942-JULY, 1945

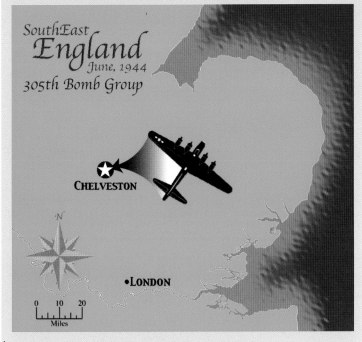

This view of a badly shot-up B-17 affords a close-up look at the aircraft fuselage call-letter positioned just aft of the starboard waist gunners window. Note that the white areas of the national insignia appear to have been subjected to a dry brush over painting of Olive Drab. This was done in an attempt to minimize the symbols serving as an aiming point for Luftwaffe pilots, a common practice among many Eighth Air Force units in the early phases of the war.

Another bit of visual trivia for the insignia buffs. The image to the left represents an early, unauthorized, combat insignia belonging to the 364th Bomb Group. This design was superseded by that seen on the facing page which was formally approved by the U.S. Army Air Force in October 1944.

In September 1943 the 422nd Bomb Squadron was removed from the 305ths' normal daylight bombing activities and assigned to special night air operations. The squadrons new duties eventually included night leaflet drops as well as pathfinder missions. Along with these new duties came a new look. The under surfaces of the squadrons B-17Fs were repainted with matt black and the normal group marker was replaced with a solid black triangle. In June of the following year most of the squadron was again re-formed into its' original roll as a daylight bombing unit. A section of the original squadron was permanently reorganized and designated as the 406th Night Leaflet Squadron. The aircraft assigned to this newly formed squadron were subsequently painted overall black while retaining a white triangle, in spite of the fact that the new unit was no longer directly assigned to the 305th Bomb Group. Eventually this marker was eliminated but the 406th NLS continued to display the original 'Double J' fuselage code of the 422nd Bomb Squadron.

The photo to the right is an excellent example of the applied 'field' use of the 305th BG combat insignia.

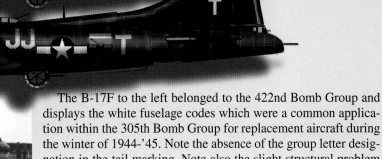

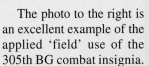

The B-17F to the left belonged to the 422nd Bomb Group and displays the white fuselage codes which were a common application within the 305th Bomb Group for replacement aircraft during the winter of 1944-'45. Note the absence of the group letter designation in the tail marking. Note also the slight structural problem with this aircraft as evidenced by the bow and wrinkled skin just above the national insignia.

40ᵀᴴ COMBAT BOMBARDMENT WING (H)

1ˢᵀ BOMBARDMENT (AIR) DIVISION

ABUNDANCE OF STRENGTH

306ᵀᴴ BOMBARDMENT GROUP (HEAVY)

In compliance with a 40th CBW directive, the group marker was additionally applied to the underside of the left wing in April 1944. Squadron colors were applied to propeller bosses, Dec.1944.

As was the case with most of the aircraft assigned to the pioneer elements of the Eighth Air Force in Great Briton, the B-17F's of the 306th received an edging treatment of medium green paint in an effort to help break up the aircrafts' profile from the air. In December 1942, 48" high light-blue squadron codes began to appear on the groups B-17's.

The group marker was introduced in June, 1943. The wing configuration was a 96" white equilateral triangle while the tail consisted of an isosceles triangle measuring 56" at the base with 72" sides. Both contained a 36" tall Insignia Blue letter 'H'. Shortly after this the call-letter was removed from the fuselage and relocated on the fin. These were 48" tall and were applied with Identification Yellow paint.

At the end of 1943 the 'H' within the group marker was converted from blue to black. March of '44 saw the arrival of the groups first consignment of natural metal finished B-17G's. The marker was applied as a black image, the letter either painted white or masked out allowing the metal to show through.

In August 1944 a horizontal 44" wide yellow band, trimmed at the top and bottom with a 2" black stripe, was added to the upper tail section of all group aircraft. At the same time, the fuselage codes were directed to be applied with black paint.The following February all codes were ordered removed from the fuselage area altogether. The familiar 48" call-letter on the tail remained.

367ᵀᴴ BMB SQDN

368ᵀᴴ BOMB SQDN

369ᵀᴴ BOMB SQDN

423ᴿᴰ BOMB SQDN

•306TH BOMBARDMENT GROUP (HEAVY)•
'ABUNDANCE OF STRENGTH'
•STATION NO.111•
THURLEIGH A/F-BEDFORDSHIRE
•CAMPAIGNS•
AIR OFFENSIVE-EUROPE • NORMANDY
NORTHERN FRANCE • RHINELAND
ARDENNES-ALSACE • CENTRAL EUROPE
•ASSIGNED EIGHTH AF•
SEPTEMBER, 1942-JULY, 1945

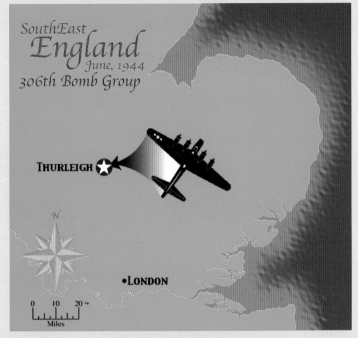

The 'Reich Wreckers' as the 306th BG was known, played a veritable game of Chinese Checkers with its' aircraft when it came to squadron codes and call-letters. These symbols appeared to jump from one location to another virtually overnight. Much of this was, of course, due to the fact that the 306th was one of the first Heavy Bombardment Groups deployed to England. As such it was subsequently subjected to all the changes, both major and minor, that were to affect all bomb groups assigned to the Eighth Air force during the course of the war. That said, a visual chronology of the 306th is nevertheless one of the more challenging of such studies in the history of the Eighth AAF. It is hoped that in spite the limited confines of this two-page spread, no earth shaking detail relating to this subject has been overlooked.

The photo below depicts two 306th Bomb Group B-17G's sometime between February and August 1944. This is determined by the lack of codes on either fuselage (ordered removed in Feb.) and the absence of the colored tail markings (ordered applied in Aug.).

In October 1942 the national insignia on some of the groups aircraft were given a 6" wide surround in Identification Yellow. At the time the 306th was expected to be transferred to North Africa for duty with the Twelfth AF. This transfer never took place and in December most of the new surrounds were treated to a quick application of insignia Blue. Many of these treatments consisted of one coat of a hastily applied over-spray which soon began to fade, often resulting in a 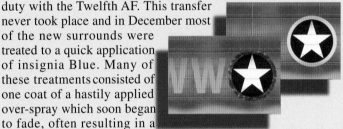 mottled blue-yellow effect. The group also began applying its' new squadron codes at this same time. These and the aircrafts' call-letter were applied to the fuselage in light blue-grey paint. The squadron codes were positioned forward the national insignia, call-letter aft. When the new 'star-and-bar' insignia was adopted in June '43, the aircraft call-letter was eventually moved to the lower tail section, while the squadron code was relocated aft of the cocarde.

On 6July44 eighteen year old Princess Elizabeth visited the 306thBG/367thBS to christened the 'Rose of York', so named in her honor. In addition to the events obvious historical significance this particular photo, taken towards the end of the ceremony, provides a good size relationship visual of the groups call-letter.

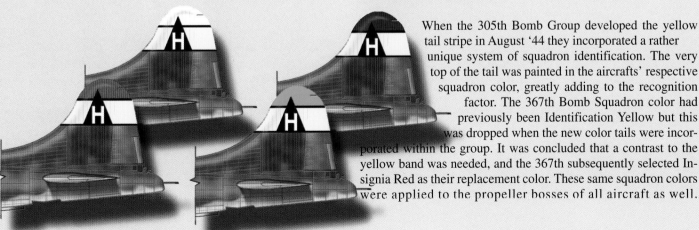

When the 305th Bomb Group developed the yellow tail stripe in August '44 they incorporated a rather unique system of squadron identification. The very top of the tail was painted in the aircrafts' respective squadron color, greatly adding to the recognition factor. The 367th Bomb Squadron color had previously been Identification Yellow but this was dropped when the new color tails were incorporated within the group. It was concluded that a contrast to the yellow band was needed, and the 367th subsequently selected Insignia Red as their replacement color. These same squadron colors were applied to the propeller bosses of all aircraft as well.

| 3RD COMBAT BOMBARDMENT WING (H) | VIII AIR SUPPORT COMMAND |  |

RECTO FACIENDO NEMINEM TIMEO

322 ND BOMBARDMENT GROUP (MEDIUM)

As far as this volume is concerned, there is little to show as marking schemes and variants for the B-26 bomber. All four medium bombardment groups were transferred from the Eighth to the Ninth Air Force in October, 1943. With the exception of the adoption of the SD110 sqdn. codes, all other unit identification devices did not begin to show up on Eighth AF bombers until nearly two months after this transfer was effected. As a result, the only real marking changes to the B-26 while with the Eighth AF were the 40 inch tall blue-grey fuselage codes, plus the adoption of the new AN-I-9a Type 3 national insignia.

131 814

ER

PN	ER	SS	DR
449TH BMB SQDN	450TH BMB SQDN	451ST BMB SQDN	452ND BMB SQDN

•322ND BOMBARDMENT GROUP (MEDIUM)•
'I FEAR NONE IN DOING RIGHT'
•STATION NO.485•
ANDREWS A/F-ESSEX
•CAMPAIGNS•
AIR OFFENSIVE-EUROPE • NORMANDY
NORTHERN FRANCE • RHINELAND
ARDENNES-ALSACE • CENTRAL EUROPE
•ASSIGNED EIGHTH AF•
DECEMBER, 1942-OCTOBER, 1943

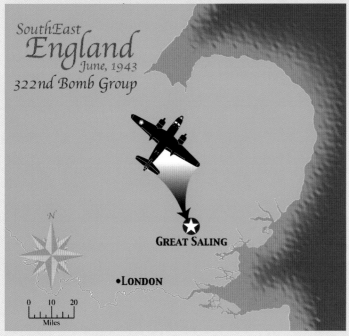

The 322nd received its' squadron codes not too long after their deployment in England. A problem from the outset was the factory positioning on the aircraft fuselage of the Type 2 national insignia. The placement of the two letter squadron code did not present any difficulty as these fit very nicely in a position just forward the of the cocarde. The single call-letter however was another matter as there was nowhere on the fuselage to place this but directly under the horizontal stabilizer. This made for poor readability under most lighting conditions, a problem that would be partially resolved somewhat at a future date.

These two ships of the 449th Bomb Squadron clearly show the problem inherent with the location of the call-letter. If the sun was not at just the right angle, the letter would be obscured by the cast shadow of the rear horizontal stabilizer.

The two photos below show the placement of squadron codes and aircraft call-letter before and adaptation of the new AN-I-9a national insignia. The first shot is of a ship belonging to the 452nd Bomb Squadron and carries what is commonly referred to as the Type 2 disk and star configuration. The second example belongs to the 449th Bomb Squadron and displays a Type 3 or 4 'star-and bars' AN-I-9a design. With this new configuration the 'bars' were often simply painted over the existing aircraft call-letter.

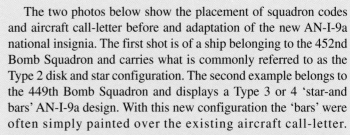

For those that enjoy World War II aircraft markings, you've got to just love this next item. If these appear to be nothing more than silhouettes of duck decoys its' because that is exactly what they are. These little fellows were sometimes painted on the nose section of 322nd Bomb Group aircraft to depict, you guessed it, *decoy missions*! From time to time the B-26 squadrons were called upon

to fly these diversionary operations on behalf of their larger cousins, the heavy bombardment groups. These missions were conducted in an attempt to confuse the Germans as to exactly when and where the real target run would be made. These flights may not have been credited as a real bombing mission but the Luftwaffe fighters and flak they encountered were certainly real enough. Consequently, someone dreamed up the idea of the little ducks as a means of crediting their often hazardous efforts. If they couldn't paint a bomb silhouette on the nose of their aircraft, they would use other means to let the world know that they were not simply sitting out the war in the local pubs. Whether these symbols were used by other units to the same end is unknown as of this writing, but the subject certainly warrants further research.

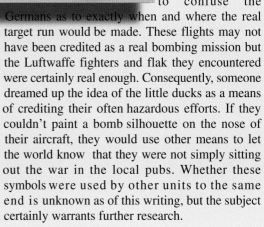

VINCAMUS SINE TIMORIS

323 RD BOMBARDMENT GROUP (MEDIUM)

As was the case with the 322nd Bomb Group, the 323rd was transfered to the Ninth Air Force before the introduction of any of the distinctive tactical markings that would later become so characteristic of the Eighth Air Force.With the exception of the transition from the Type2 to the Type3 national insignia, the only other visual modification to the 323rds' aircraft was the application in a blue-grey paint of the 40" tall SD110 squadron codes to the rear fuselage area.

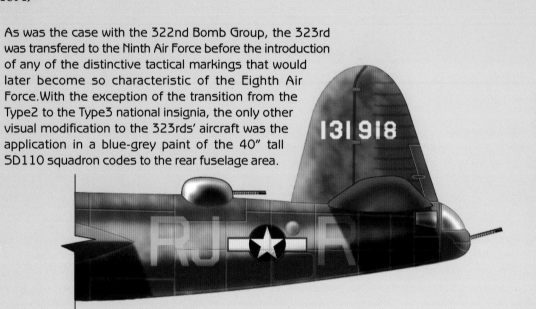

453RD BMB SQDN

454TH BMB SQDN

455TH BMB SQDN

456TH BMB SQDN

•323RD BOMBARDMENT GROUP (MEDIUM)•
'WITHOUT FEAR WE CONQUER'
•STATION NO.119•
HORHAM A/F-SUFFOLK
•STATION NO.358•
EARLS COLNE A/F-ESSEX
•CAMPAIGNS•
AIR OFFENSIVE-EUROPE • NORMANDY
NORTHERN FRANCE • RHINELAND
ARDENNES-ALSACE • CENTRAL EUROPE
•ASSIGNED EIGHTH AF•
MAY, 1943-OCTOBER, 1943

The photo above clearly illustrates the visibility problems inherent with the fuselage call-letter on the B-26 Medium Bomber. This image's proximity to the rear horizontal stabilizer virtually guaranteed that it would spend much of the time in shadow. If there exists a logical explanation as to why the call-letter was not simply positioned on the fin/rudder area, that explanation is as yet forthcoming.

A typical scenario with all B-26 bombardment units during this period was to allow the 'bars' of the new AN-I-9a national insignia to overlap the existing fuselage call-letter in the process of applying the replacement national symbol. As these letters were already tucked almost completely under the rear horizontal stabilizers, there was precious little alternate space in which to relocate the them. Over-painting was thus deemed the most expeditious means of affecting the adoption of the new insignia. With the subsequent arrival of replacement aircraft, the problem of the factory applied national insignia was resolved, at least to the extent that the call-letter no longer came into direct conflict with this image during the painting process.

The shot below was actually taken at a slightly later time period than that dealt with in this particular volume. It was in fact taken after the 323rd Bomb Group had been transferred to the Ninth Air Force. However, the image of the 455th Bomb Squadron insignia on the nose of this aircraft was just too tempting to pass up.

The photo to the left shows the original application of the recently adopted SD110 squadron codes, and serves to illustrate the space limitations inherent with the medium bomber fuselage.

351ST BOMBARDMENT GROUP (HEAVY)

The 351st group marker was introduced in June, 1943. This called for the application to the tail of a white 72" equilateral and a similar 96" triangle to the upper right wing. Both of these symbols were to contain a Insignia Blue letter 'J' approximately 48" in height, however Identification Yellow was substituted in a limited number of initial applications. A 36" tall yellow call-letter was additionally directed to be located on the tail, just below the aircraft serial number.

The 351st was assigned its' squadron codes shortly after their deployment in England. These were applied to either side of the groups aircraft as 48" tall, light blue-grey letters. The paint on these codes had barely dried when the new AN-I-9a 'star-and-bars' national insignia was introduced. The new insignia was painted on allowing the leading bar to obscure part of the second letter of the squadron code.

The group marker was modified to a white letter on black triangle with receipt of natural metal finished B-17Gs' in March 1944.

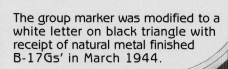

August 1944 saw the introduction of the groups high visibility color tail markings. This consisted of a 48" wide red stripe applied diagonally across the surface of the tail section. These applications varied greatly, with some examples exhibiting painstakingly masked out call-letters and serial number while others simply over painted and 'block masked' over the existing graphic images..

508TH BMB SQDN

509TH BMB SQDN

510TH BMB SQDN

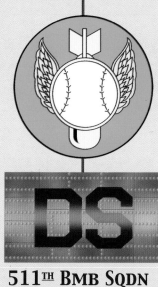

511TH BMB SQDN

•351ST BOMBARDMENT GROUP (HEAVY)•
•STATION NO.110•
POLEBROOK A/F-NORTHAMPTONSHIRE
•CAMPAIGNS•
AIR OFFENSIVE-EUROPE • NORMANDY
NORTHERN FRANCE • RHINELAND
ARDENNES-ALSACE • CENTRAL EUROPE
•ASSIGNED EIGHTH AF•
MAY, 1943-JUNE, 1945

This PR shot of Clark Gable at the port side waist gun station shows the close proximity of the aircraft call-letter to this position. In early 1944 this policy was amended and the call-letter was repositioned further back on the fuselage. (refer to photo directly below)

The 351st, it may be remembered, was the group to which Gable was assigned for his nine month long filming of 'Combat America' which he produced on behalf of the Army Air Force.

This shot gives a good look at all the group and squadron marking components of the 351stBG. An interesting foot note regarding this B-17G and the B-17F in the photo directly below this one. Upon close examination of these images, it can be determined that both of these ships display identical squadron markings. Even without the aid of a detailed aircraft manifest for the 351stBG, one can correctly surmise that the uppermost of the two images is that of a replacement. Key features to look for (a.) the presence or lack of camouflage (b.) the serial number, in particular the first digit (c.) the existence or lack of a group marker (d.) if present, the color of the group marker (e.) the existence of color scheme on the tail (f) last but certainly not least, the configuration of the national insignia. These are the basic elements to consider when scrutinizing WWII USAAF World War II aircraft photos.

Three of the 351st Bomb Group squadrons developed an interesting means of identifying flight leaders within their respective units. The illustrations below depict those devises as used by the 509th, 510th and 511th Bomb Squadrons. It is not known why the 508th Bomb Squadron did not employ a similar graphic devise with which to distinguish its' own flight leaders.

This might appear to be simply another, somewhat underexposed, example of 351st Bomb Group markings. Upon closer examination of this photo however, an interesting detail can be discerned, one easily overlooked by a cursory glance. The small white object on the rudder is not a dust spot, or imperfection in the film. It is in fact a triangle, a squadron marker such as depicted in the illustration at left, which denotes this ship as a flight leader belonging to the 509th Bomb Squadron.

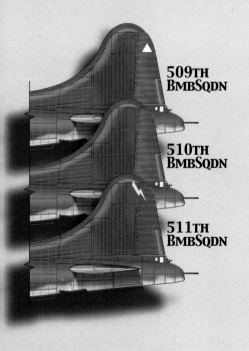

509TH BMBSQDN

510TH BMBSQDN

511TH BMBSQDN

41ST COMBAT BOMBARDMENT WING (H)

1ST BOMBARDMENT (AIR) DIVISION

379TH BOMBARDMENT GROUP (HEAVY)

POTESTAS ACCURATIOQUE

The new SD110 squadron codes were applied to 379th BG B-17Fs' almost immediately after their arrival in England. The original directive called for 36" tall light blue-grey letters but this color selection was amended to Insignia White the following November, better visibility being sited as the motivating factor. An additional call-letter was applied to the tail in either yellow or white paint.

The 379th group marker was assigned in June and called for a 72" equilateral Insignia White triangle incorporating an Insignia Blue letter 'K'. This was directed to be applied to both the fin and upper right wing surfaces. This became a white letter on black triangle and black fuselage letter codes with receipt of natural metal finished B-17Gs'.

In August 1944 all existing group markers were ordered removed from all 379th aircraft and replaced with 10' equilateral triangle comprised of 24" wide yellow bands. Contained and centered therein a standard sized black group marker with white letter 'K'.

With the adoption of the high-visibility tail markings, the 379th dispensed with SD110 fuselage codes. Instead a number at the apex of the triangle denoted squadron assignment. i.e.:
1 = 524th Bmb Sqdn
2 = 525th Bmb Sqdn
3 = 526th Bmb Sqdn
4 = 527th Bmb sqdn

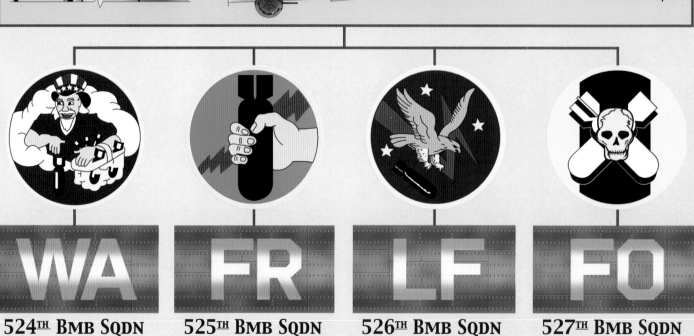

524TH BMB SQDN **525TH BMB SQDN** **526TH BMB SQDN** **527TH BMB SQDN**

•379TH BOMBARDMENT GROUP (HEAVY)•
'POWER AND ACCURACY'
•STATION NO.117•
KIMBOLTON A/F-HUNTINGDONSHIRE
•CAMPAIGNS•
AIR OFFENSIVE-EUROPE • NORMANDY
NORTHERN FRANCE • RHINELAND
ARDENNES-ALSACE • CENTRAL EUROPE
•ASSIGNED EIGHTH AF•
MAY, 1943-JUNE, 1945

An excellent example of early UK deployment markings of the 379th BG. The Type 2 national insignia coupled with the SD110 squadron codes narrow the time frame of this photo as between May and June, 1943. It was in June '43 that the 379th was assigned its' Triangle 'K' group marker.

The absence of any fuselage codes in the image below indicate that this photo was probably taken sometime after August, 1944. It was at that time that the 379th discontinued the use SD110 codes after adopting the new high-visibility tail marking system.

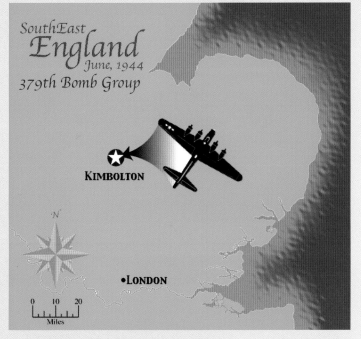

As if they didn't already have enough to do getting the units aircraft battle ready, the ground crews of the 379th Bomb Group had no sooner arrived at their duty station when they were inundated with a barrage of cosmetic changes to the groups B-17Fs'. In rapid succession they first had to apply the newly assigned SD110 squadron codes and call-letters, immediately after which came the new AN-I-9a national insignia change, followed in short order by the Triangle 'K' group marker. These guys should have received some sort of medal for these efforts alone.

In addition to being a interesting combat photo, the shot below provides a good visual reference as to the size and positioning of the first pattern, blue on white 379th Bomb Group marker.

This non injury crash (crew bailout) in Denmark affords a good close-up look at the marking detail of the entire port side empennage assembly. Of special note in this photo, the last two digits of the aircraft serial number overlapping onto the rudder.

1ST COMBAT BOMBARDMENT WING (H)

1ST BOMBARDMENT (AIR) DIVISION

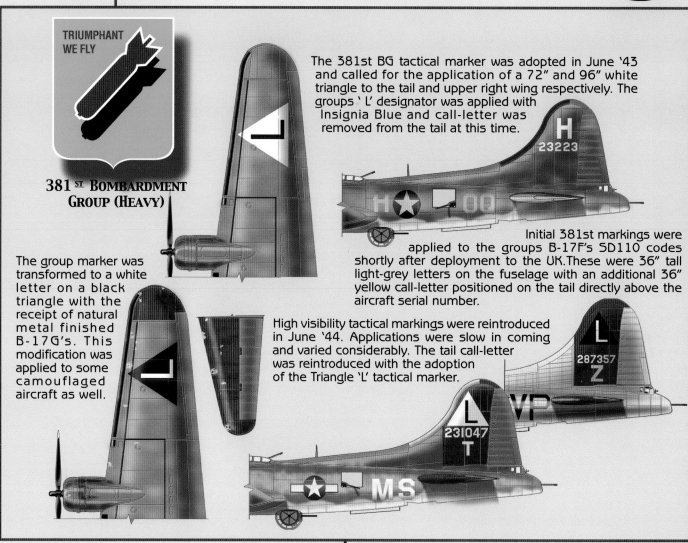

TRIUMPHANT WE FLY

381ST BOMBARDMENT GROUP (HEAVY)

The 381st BG tactical marker was adopted in June '43 and called for the application of a 72" and 96" white triangle to the tail and upper right wing respectively. The groups ' L' designator was applied with Insignia Blue and call-letter was removed from the tail at this time.

The group marker was transformed to a white letter on a black triangle with the receipt of natural metal finished B-17G's. This modification was applied to some camouflaged aircraft as well.

Initial 381st markings were applied to the groups B-17F's 5D110 codes shortly after deployment to the UK. These were 36" tall light-grey letters on the fuselage with an additional 36" yellow call-letter positioned on the tail directly above the aircraft serial number.

High visibility tactical markings were reintroduced in June '44. Applications were slow in coming and varied considerably. The tail call-letter was reintroduced with the adoption of the Triangle 'L' tactical marker.

532ND BMB SQDN

533RD BMB SQDN

534TH BMB SQDN

535TH BMB SQDN

•381st Bombardment Group (Heavy)•
'Triumphant We Fly'
•Station No.167•
Ridgewell A/F–Essex
•Campaigns•
Air Offensive-Europe • Normandy
Northern France • Rhineland
Ardennes-Alsace • Central Europe
•Assigned Eighth AF•
June, 1943-June, 1945

SouthEast
England
June, 1944
381st Bomb Group

RIDGEWELL

•LONDON

0 10 20
Miles

The above example tends to make one ask his-or-herself; 'Is there any power on earth that would compel me to leave the ground in this aircraft?' Nevertheless this photo affords a good look at almost every tactical marking modification 381st BG aircraft underwent. Ignoring the oil leaks and patch work, note the variations in the national insignia and the color difference of the tail and wing markings.

A good look at the 381st BGs' original tactical configuration shortly after the groups arrival in Great Britain.

Changes to the 381st BG tactical markings were numerous and came in rapid succession during that units initial phases of deployment in England. Unique among these changes was the replacement of previously issued SD110 codes for the 533rd, 534th and 535th Bomb Squadrons, the only such recorded code modification to an Eighth Army Air Force unit while based in the UK. No sooner had the ground crews finished applying the first allocated codes when they were ordered to remove and replace them with another set of letters. Added to this activity was the change of national insignia the very month of the groups arrival. Coupled with normal maintenance and refits for combat readiness, it's not hard to image a lot of weary, disgruntled ground crewmen.

This rare war era color photo shows all elements of the 381st Bomb Groups second pattern tactical markings including the application to the upper right wing surface.

At left is an example of the first pattern tactical markings for the 381st BG. Note the second issue 'MS' squadron code on the two trailing aircraft.

41ST COMBAT BOMBARDMENT WING (H)

1ST BOMBARDMENT (AIR) DIVISION

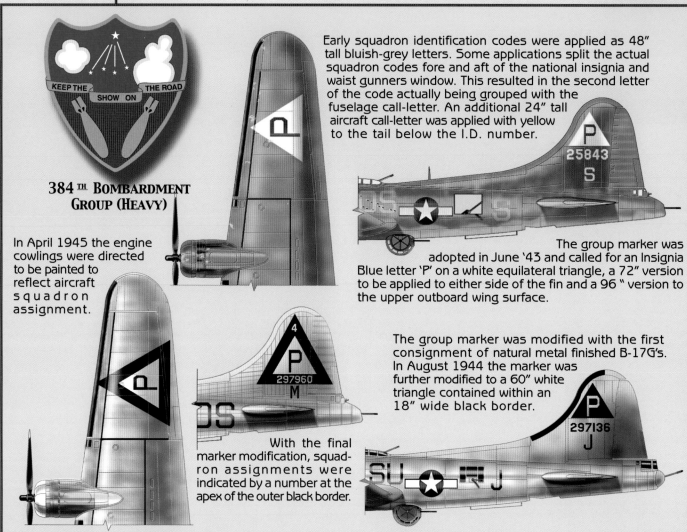

384TH BOMBARDMENT GROUP (HEAVY)

KEEP THE SHOW ON THE ROAD

Early squadron identification codes were applied as 48" tall bluish-grey letters. Some applications split the actual squadron codes fore and aft of the national insignia and waist gunners window. This resulted in the second letter of the code actually being grouped with the fuselage call-letter. An additional 24" tall aircraft call-letter was applied with yellow to the tail below the I.D. number.

In April 1945 the engine cowlings were directed to be painted to reflect aircraft squadron assignment.

The group marker was adopted in June '43 and called for an Insignia Blue letter 'P' on a white equilateral triangle, a 72" version to be applied to either side of the fin and a 96 " version to the upper outboard wing surface.

The group marker was modified with the first consignment of natural metal finished B-17G's. In August 1944 the marker was further modified to a 60" white triangle contained within an 18" wide black border.

With the final marker modification, squadron assignments were indicated by a number at the apex of the outer black border.

544TH BMB SQDN

545TH BMB SQDN

546TH BMB SQDN

547TH BMB SQDN

•384TH BOMBARDMENT GROUP (HEAVY)•
'KEEP THE SHOW ON THE ROAD'
•STATION NO.106•
GRAFTON UNDERWOOD A/F–NORTHAMPTONSHIRE
•CAMPAIGNS•
AIR OFFENSIVE–EUROPE • NORMANDY
NORTHERN FRANCE • RHINELAND
ARDENNES–ALSACE • CENTRAL EUROPE
•ASSIGNED EIGHTH AF•
MAY, 1943–JUNE, 1945

An early example of 384th BG first pattern tactical markings. Note that the red outline on the national insignia has been over-painted with blue pursuant to the modification order of Sept.'43.

With receipt of all natural metal finished B-17G's, the 384th BG marker was converted to a white-on-black pattern image.

If one were to sit down and begin sorting through a stack of wartime photographs of the 384th Bomb Group, a general lack of continuity in the application of SD110 squadron codes becomes quickly apparent. These codes were split, combined and staggered on the groups' aircraft fuselages in almost any configuration imaginable. There appears to have been no firm directive issued pertaining to the matter of specific placement of the individual code components, legibility being the sole dominating factor. As a result of this policy, we have today, a fascinating array of photographic material to study in a vain attempt to determine just which configuration constitutes 'the norm'.

These two photos provide an excellent look at the final group marking configurations for the 384th Bomb Group. Both of these are 'text book' applications of the tactical marking devises adopted by the group in the last eight months of the war. Note the squadron assignment numbers at the apex of each outer black triangle.

385TH BOMBARDMENT GROUP (HEAVY)

ALES VICTORIA

The first group markers were applied to tail and upper right wing as a yellow letter 'G' on a light grey background. By mid summer '43, specifications modified this image from Identification Yellow to an Insignia Blue letter, approximately 40" tall. The directive called for a white background but grey continued to be applied on some aircraft. Wing applications generally consisted of a 72"X 57" rectangle with a 45" letter.

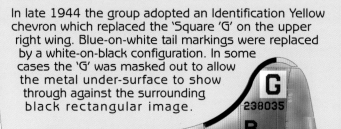

By the end of 1943, all 385th aircraft displayed propeller bosses painted in assigned sqdn. colors.

Yellow call-letters were applied to tail sections. Position varied greatly and letter sizes ranged from between 24" and 48" in height. On some aircraft a 36" tall blue-grey call-letter was painted on the fuselage, just aft the waist gunners window.

In late 1944 the group adopted an Identification Yellow chevron which replaced the 'Square 'G' on the upper right wing. Blue-on-white tail markings were replaced by a white-on-black configuration. In some cases the 'G' was masked out to allow the metal under-surface to show through against the surrounding black rectangular image.

The 385th BG gradually discontinued the application of the additional fuselage call-letter prior to its' transfer from the 4th CBW to the 93rd CBW.

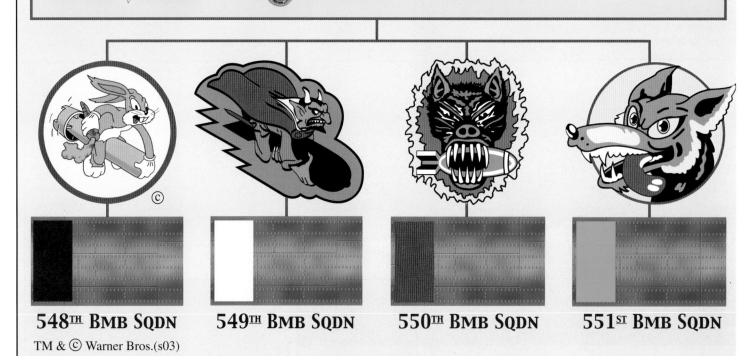

548TH BMB SQDN   **549TH BMB SQDN**   **550TH BMB SQDN**   **551ST BMB SQDN**

•385TH BOMBARDMENT GROUP (HEAVY)•
'WINGED VICTORY'
•STATION NO.155•
GREAT ASHFIELD A/F–SUFFOLK
•CAMPAIGNS•
AIR OFFENSIVE–EUROPE • NORMANDY
NORTHERN FRANCE • RHINELAND
ARDENNES–ALSACE • CENTRAL EUROPE
•ASSIGNED EIGHTH AF•
JUNE, 1943–AUGUST, 1944

Aside from the obvious drama inherent with this photo, the image provides an exceptional close-up view of the application of tactical markings to the tail of a 385th Bomb Group aircraft.

SouthEast
England
June, 1944
385th Bomb Group

GREAT ASHFIELD

•LONDON

N

0 10 20
Miles

Part of the 385th Bomb Groups history that tends to be a bit confusing centers around this units transfer to the 93rd Combat Bombardment Wing during the final months of the European conflict. This transfer, effected in February 1945, necessitated a complete cosmetic make-over, the result of which presents an entirely different visual appearance than that previously associated with the group. Gone altogether was the familiar Square 'G' configuration so often associated with the 385th.

The photo to the immediate right and the graphics below illustrate the 'face lift' that aircraft of the 385th underwent subsequent to that units transfer to the 93rd CBW.

The overhead photo below clearly shows the application of a first pattern 385th tactical marker to the right wing. Note the national insignia on the left wing and what appears to possibly be a yellow contour outline.

The photo at left depicts a second generation, first pattern tactical marking configuration, as applied to 385th BG natural metal finished replacement aircraft.

3RD COMBAT BOMBARDMENT WING (H)

VIII AIR SUPPORT COMMAND

386 TH BOMBARDMENT GROUP (MEDIUM)

The biggest problem inherent with the B-26 fuselage, at least from a tactical marking point of view, was the extremely limited surface area to which such devises could be affixed. This problem was compounded with the adoption of the revised national insignia featuring the addition of 'bars' on each side of the roundel. This necessitated placing the 40" light-grey call-letter partially under the rear wing, obscuring this image under many natural lighting conditions.

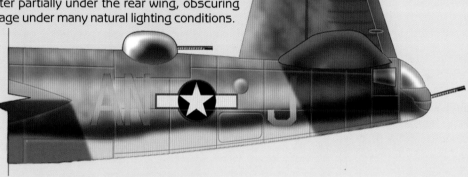

552ND BMB SQDN

553RD BMB SQDN

554TH BMB SQDN

555TH BMB SQDN

•386th Bombardment Group (Medium)•
'The Crusaders'
•Station No.150•
Boxted A/F-Essex
•Campaigns•
**Air Offensive-Europe • Normandy
Northern France • Rhineland
Ardennes-Alsace • Central Europe**
•Assigned Eighth AF•
June, 1943-June-1945

The two photographs below provide a fairly good look at both the port and starboard application of tactical markings for the B-26 Marauder. By closely comparing the two images it becomes immediately apparent just how sensitive to light the blue-grey fuselage codes really were. It requires a second closer look to read these markings in the upper photo, however, the lower image presents the viewer with an entirely different vision of these same fuselage codes. Even allowing for variables in film processing techniques and exposure values, it is clear that ambient light direction played an important role when it came to tactical marking legibility.

This shot gives a good partial close-up look at the tactical fuselage markings of a ship belonging to the 554th Bomb Squadron. This, by the way, was the accepted method for resupplying fifty caliber ammunition to the rear waist gunners station.

From a tactical marking standpoint there were two items that affected the 386th Bomb Group soon after their deployment to England. The redesign of the national insignia (discussed on the previous page) and the issuing of the groups new SD110 squadron codes and individual aircraft call-letters. Even though the new 'star-and-bar' insignia repositioned the call-letter virtually under the horizontal stabilizers, this was not the total detriment that a similar application might have had on one of this aircrafts' larger counterparts. Being a smaller and far more maneuverable aircraft than either the B-17 or B-24, the Marauder was able to fly in much tighter bombing formations than their larger cousins. This made air-to-air recognition a much easier proposition due to the reduced distance between one ship and another. The diagram at right represents a typical B-26 bombing formation. The Marauder did not posses the defensive firepower of the heavy bombers and it thus became even more essential to maintain as tight of formation as possible to protect themselves from enemy fighters. Being somewhat more agile, the B-26 Marauder did have a slight advantage over the heavy bombers in its' ability to take evasive maneuvers after completing the bombing run.

FORMATION LEADER

WINGMAN   **WINGMAN**

DEPUTY FORMATION LEADER

WINGMAN   **WINGMAN**

FLIGHT LEADER   **FLIGHT LEADER**

WINGMAN   **WINGMAN**   **WINGMAN**   **WINGMAN**

DEPUTY FLIGHT LEADER   **DEPUTY FLIGHT LEADER**

WINGMAN   **WINGMAN**   **WINGMAN**   **WINGMAN**

3RD COMBAT BOMBARDMENT WING (H)

VIII AIR SUPPORT COMMAND

387TH BOMBARDMENT GROUP (MEDIUM)

Like the other three medium bomb groups assigned early on to the Eighth Air Force, the 387th was not with the Eighth long enough to have any of that organizations tactical marking patterns or high-visibility color schemes assigned to it. As with its' sister squadron, the 386th, the transition from Type2 to Type3 national insignia and the adoption of 40" blue-grey fuselage codes were the only two marking modifications the 387th underwent while still assigned to the Eighth.

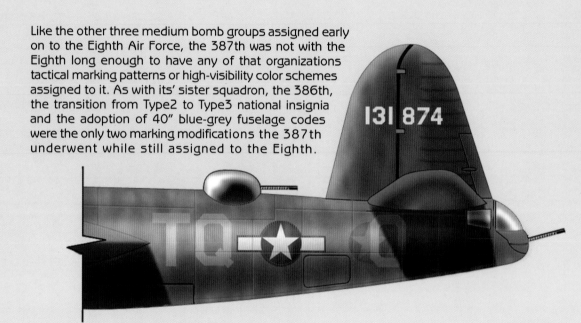

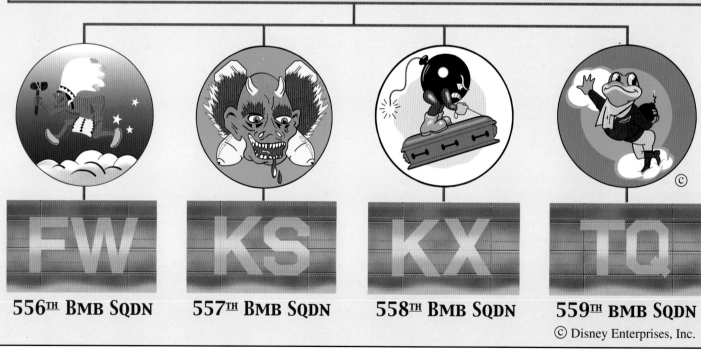

556TH BMB SQDN   **557TH BMB SQDN**   **558TH BMB SQDN**   **559TH BMB SQDN**

•387th Bombardment Group (Medium)•
•Station No.162•
Chipping Ongar A/F-Essex
•Campaigns•
Air Offensive-Europe • Normandy
Northern France • Rhineland
Ardennes-Alsace • Central Europe
•Assigned Eighth AF•
June, 1943-October, 1943

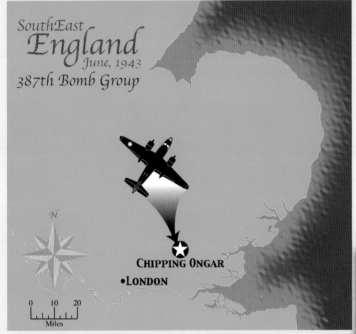

Close scrutiny of the photograph directly below reveals the 'KS' signature SD110 code of the 557th Bomb Squadron. The aircraft call-letter 'H' is barely legible in the shadow of the horizontal stabilizer. Of particular interest in this photo is the over-painted Type2 national insignia just aft the squadron code. It is a fairly safe supposition that this shot can be dated to the summer of nineteen forty three, and that this aircraft would soon be displaying the recently adopted, red outlined, AN-I-9a 'star-and-bars' national insignia.

On page seventy-three the close formation flying inherent with the medium bomber was discussed. A problem relating to the legibility of individual call-letters on the B-26 was the result of this image being partially obscured by the cast shadow of the rear horizontal stabilizer. For unknown reasons it was decided to place both the SD110 squadron code as well as the individual aircraft call-letter on the limited rear fuselage surface area of the Marauder. When this aircraft carried the older Type2 national insignia, this arrangement did not present to much of a problem. This changed however with the introduction of the new AN-I-9a 'star-and-bars'. Relocating the call-letter to the vertical tail would seemed to have been a logical alternate choice. It appears however that the powers-that-be liked these symbols on the fuselage and there they remained for the rest of the war. The problem of legibility was minimized somewhat by the close proximity of these aircraft to each other once in an attack formation. The photo to the immediate right serves to illustrate just how close a distance this really was. Although this particular shot is of the 449th Squadron of the 322nd Bomb Group, it provides an excellent close-up look at a typical combat formation of Eighth Air Force medium bombers during World War II.

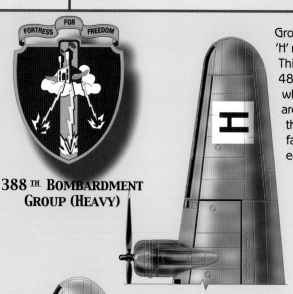

388TH BOMBARDMENT GROUP (HEAVY)

Ground crews began applying the newly assigned Square 'H' marker shortly after the 388ths' deployment to England. This called for a 36" Insignia Blue letter centered on a 48"-60" white square, the tail size varied depending on whether a particular application overlapped the rudder area. There were some complaints regarding the 'high- bar H' configuration due to the fact that at a distance this symbol was easily mistaken for the letter 'M'.

The application of a 24" call-letter to the tail in Identification Yellow was the only additional cosmetic alteration that 388th ground crews had to concern themselves with. As usual, the arrival of natural metal finished B-17Gs' saw the transformation of the marker to a white or metal see-through against a black square.

In early 1945 the 388th adopted parallel black bands in compliance with 45th CBW directives. Wing configurations consisted of twin 36" bands with a 60" separation. Tail applications generally held to a 36" lower band combined with a 30" upper band that ascended from the bottom of the marker.

A 28" tall white call-letter was centered below the I.D. number.

560TH BMB SQDN

561ST BMB SQDN

562ND BMB SQDN

563RD BMB SQDN

•388TH BOMBARDMENT GROUP (HEAVY)•
'FORTRESS FOR FREEDOM"
•STATION NO.136•
KNETTISHALL A/F-SUFFOLK
•CAMPAIGNS•
AIR OFFENSIVE-EUROPE • NORMANDY
NORTHERN FRANCE • RHINELAND
ARDENNES-ALSACE • CENTRAL EUROPE
•ASSIGNED EIGHTH AF•
JUNE, 1943-JUNE, 1945

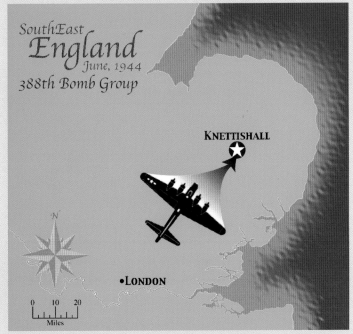

This amazing combat photo shows what appears to be a Junkers JU88 twin engine fighter completing a strafing pass on a 388th Bomb Group B-17. The JU88 was a formidable opponent of allied bomber crews and was a particular nemesis of British airmen as this aircraft was Germanys' principle night fighter. Although shot at an extremely oblique angle, the Square 'H' group marker is nevertheless still discernible at the far end of the wing surface. The shinning area just this side of the marker may well be recently sustained battle damage, possibly a bullet hole received from the JU88.

Buried deep within some long overlooked file may be the answer as to why the 388th BG was never assigned SD110 squadron codes. There were several long serving units in the Eighth Air Force that applied their codes inconsistently (i.e. the 385th Bomb Group) but the 388th was never even allocated squadron identification codes. This situation would prevail throughout this units entire combat tour deployment. Whether or not this was a simple matter of bureaucratic oversight is another of those small WWII mysteries that persists to this day. In retrospect it makes one wonder just how important these codes were in the first place, the 388th seems to have gotten along just fine without them.

Here is yet one more example that illustrates the unfortunate fact that the majority of war time photos' primarily focused on an aircrafts' tail section after a crash landing or runway mishap. This shot provides an excellent view of the 388ths' high-visibility tactical tail marking configuration.

This photograph is an excellent representation of a 388th Bomb Group 'transition period' aircraft. Beginning in March of 1944 the 388th began receiving replacement B-17G's devoid of any factory applied paint. These all natural metal finished ships received basically the same tactical marking scheme as their camouflaged predecessors. The white rectangle displayed on both the tail and wing however, became black images containing a white letter. On numerous applications the 'H' was simply masked out prior to applying the black 'square'. Once the mask was removed the metal under surface shone through thus eliminating the need for a second application of paint to create the letter therein.

389TH BOMBARDMENT GROUP (HEAVY)

In August 1943 the 389th adopted a white disc with blue letter 'C' as its group marker. The disc varied in size ranging from between 69" to 72" in diameter, with an average letter height of approximately 36".

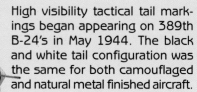

Upon their return from temporary duty in North Africa, it was some weeks before all group aircraft had their national insignia brought into compliance with standard Eighth Air Force requirements. In the interim, an Identification Yellow contour outline was much in evidence on many of the groups veteran B-24's.

In March 1944 the 389th received its' SD110 squadron codes. Initially applied to the fuselage of natural metal finish B-17G's using Identification Yellow, this was quickly amended to Black. Light blue-grey was used to apply the codes to the groups camouflaged aircraft.

High visibility tactical tail markings began appearing on 389th B-24's in May 1944. The black and white tail configuration was the same for both camouflaged and natural metal finished aircraft.

564TH BMB SQDN

565TH BMB SQDN

566TH BMB SQDN

567TH BMB SQDN

•389th Bombardment Group (Heavy)•
'The Sky Scorpions'
•Station No.114•
Hethel A/F-Norfolk
•Campaigns•
Air Offensive-Europe • Normandy
Northern France • Rhineland
Ardennes-Alsace • Central Europe
•Assigned Eighth AF•
June, 1943-June, 1945

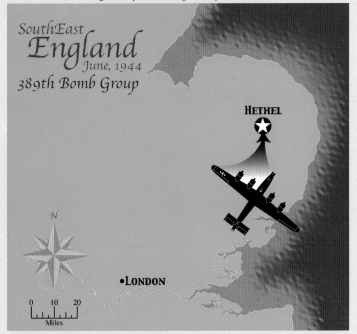

SouthEast *England* June, 1944 389th Bomb Group

HETHEL

•LONDON

0 10 20
Miles

The B-24's of the 389th Bomb Group initially entered into combat operations in a somewhat undressed state, as it were. With the exception of the serial number, the only additional tail adornment consisted of a 28-30 inch tall call-letter. Like other B-24 units (such as the 93rd Bomb Group) that saw combat in the Mediterranean, the 389th displayed the RAF flashes on their aircrafts fin area, a cus-

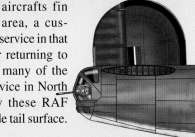

tom so often associated with service in that theater of operations. After returning to England for the last time, many of the groups aircraft that saw service in North Africa continued to carry these RAF flashes repainted on the inside tail surface.

Of particular interest in this photograph is the national insignia displayed on the fuselage. The normally white areas have been dulled to a light-grey, an modification technique first adopted in October 1942. The outline appears to be an application of Identification Yellow which would indicate that this aircraft may well have seen service with the groups detachment to North Africa.

Although initially assigned to the Eighth Air Force in June of 1943, a contingent from the 389th was detached to Libya for a stint of combat in the Mediterranean Theater beginning in July, 1943. While so deployed the detachment participated in the now famous low-level attack against the Polesti oil fields of Rumania on 1Aug43. The detachment returned to England for a brief period before finding themselves TDY once again, this time to Tunisia. In October of 1943 the entire group was reunited once again at their permanent base in South East England. It was about this time that the original system of aircraft call-letters underwent their first modification since the groups initial arrival in Great Britain. The top right image depicts the original use of bar codes as employed by the 389th from August until November, 1943. The 564th and 564th Bomb Groups used no additional symbols with their call-letters at this time. The middle panel represents the revised call-letters adopted in November '43. The 565th Squadron it will be noted now employed the use of a bar symbol, the 564th remaining the sole holdout and did not in fact ever adopt an additional symbol as a means of unit identification. With the introduction of High-visibility tactical tail markings in May of 1944, the somewhat narrow white tail stripe made it necessary to once again modify the call-letter system. This modification was slight however, resulting in a simple vertical relocation of the existing symbols.

| 566THBS | –A |
| 567THBS | –Z |

565THBS	–Z
566THBS	A+
567THBS	Z–

565THBS	Z̄
566THBS	A+
567THBS	Z̲

The two photographs directly above are prime examples of both the first and second pattern tactical marking schemes for the 389th Bomb Group. The combination of call-letter and symbol on the tail plus the SD110 fuselage code contained in the lower photo clearly identifies this ship as belonging to the 567th Bomb Squadron.

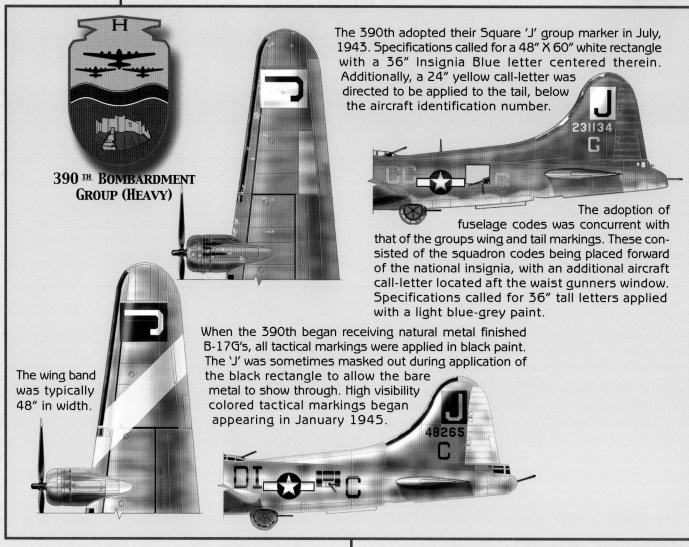

390TH BOMBARDMENT GROUP (HEAVY)

The 390th adopted their Square 'J' group marker in July, 1943. Specifications called for a 48" X 60" white rectangle with a 36" Insignia Blue letter centered therein. Additionally, a 24" yellow call-letter was directed to be applied to the tail, below the aircraft identification number.

The adoption of fuselage codes was concurrent with that of the groups wing and tail markings. These consisted of the squadron codes being placed forward of the national insignia, with an additional aircraft call-letter located aft the waist gunners window. Specifications called for 36" tall letters applied with a light blue-grey paint.

The wing band was typically 48" in width.

When the 390th began receiving natural metal finished B-17G's, all tactical markings were applied in black paint. The 'J' was sometimes masked out during application of the black rectangle to allow the bare metal to show through. High visibility colored tactical markings began appearing in January 1945.

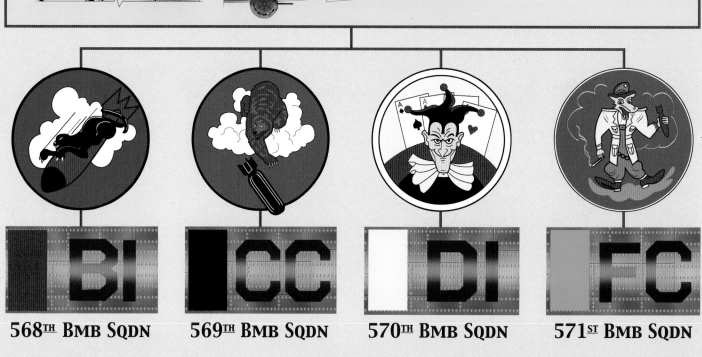

568TH BMB SQDN

569TH BMB SQDN

570TH BMB SQDN

571ST BMB SQDN

•390th Bombardment Group (Heavy)•
'Wing On! Three Ninetieth'
•Station No.153•
PARHAM-FRAMLINGHAM A/F-SUFFOLK
•Campaigns•
AIR OFFENSIVE-EUROPE • NORMANDY
NORTHERN FRANCE • RHINELAND
ARDENNES-ALSACE • CENTRAL EUROPE
•Assigned Eighth AF•
JULY, 1943-JUNE, 1945

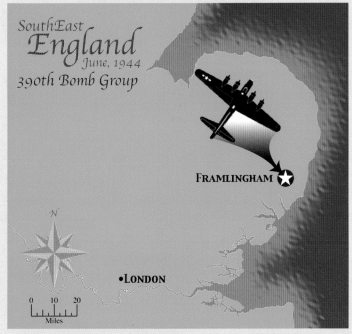

The top two mission photos display typical tactical marking patterns of the 390th BG.

Beginning in July 1944 all squadrons comprising the 390thBG adopted the policy of applying a 12" band of color to the aircrafts forward nose area.

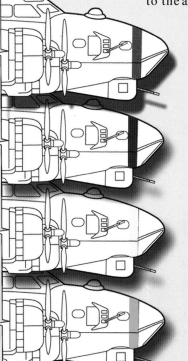

568th Bomb Squadron

569th Bomb Squadron

570thBomb squadron

571st Bomb Squadron

One of, if not the single most famous aerial combat photo to come out of World War II is the image seen below. This was taken on the twenty-seventh of September, 1943 on a rain against the port facilities at Emden, Germany. This was the seventeenth combat mission for the 390th Bomb Group and the drama of this scene captured the attention of America. It took some years after the war to narrow down the specifics surrounding this photo, but with the aid of more contemporary technology, the details concerning this

particular mission are now pretty much established. The fact that this was a photo concerning the 390th was never an issue, thanks to the Square 'J' tail marking on the B-17F in the lower center of the format. The question became not one of 'what' but of 'when and where'. Although not legible in this photo, recent computer enhancement techniques were able to pull up additional tactical images affixed to the fuselage of the aforementioned aircraft. An uppercase letter 'F' appears not only on the rear fuselage but on the nose area near the gun station. Putting this information together with other previously known factors, researchers were finally able to assign specific data to this important visual image of the Eighth Air Force World War Two.

Looking at these black and white images today, it is perfectly understandable why for so long after the war few individuals removed from the actual theater of operations realized the full use of color involved in the identification process of the Eighth Army Air Force bomb groups.

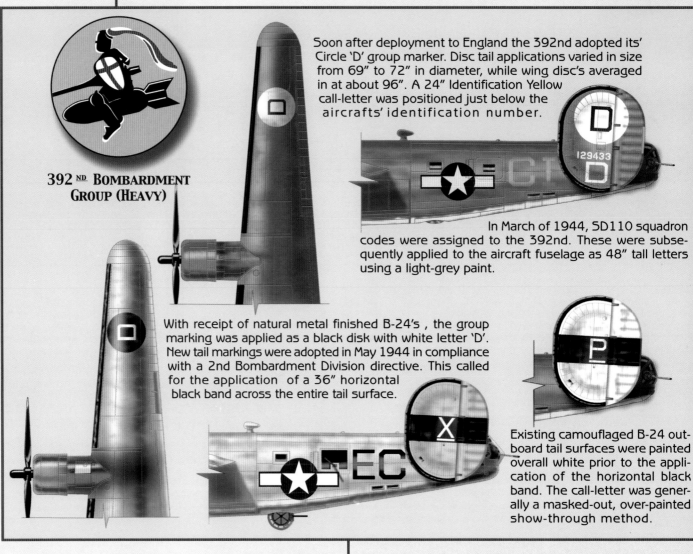

392ND BOMBARDMENT GROUP (HEAVY)

Soon after deployment to England the 392nd adopted its' Circle 'D' group marker. Disc tail applications varied in size from 69" to 72" in diameter, while wing disc's averaged in at about 96". A 24" Identification Yellow call-letter was positioned just below the aircrafts' identification number.

129433

In March of 1944, SD110 squadron codes were assigned to the 392nd. These were subsequently applied to the aircraft fuselage as 48" tall letters using a light-grey paint.

With receipt of natural metal finished B-24's , the group marking was applied as a black disk with white letter 'D'. New tail markings were adopted in May 1944 in compliance with a 2nd Bombardment Division directive. This called for the application of a 36" horizontal black band across the entire tail surface.

Existing camouflaged B-24 outboard tail surfaces were painted overall white prior to the application of the horizontal black band. The call-letter was generally a masked-out, over-painted show-through method.

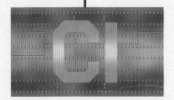

576TH BMB SQDN

577TH BMB SQDN

578TH BMB SQDN

579TH BMB SQDN

•392ND BOMBARDMENT GROUP (HEAVY)•
•STATION NO.118•
WENDLING A/F-NORFOLK
•CAMPAIGNS•
AIR OFFENSIVE-EUROPE • NORMANDY
NORTHERN FRANCE • RHINELAND
ARDENNES-ALSACE • CENTRAL EUROPE
•ASSIGNED EIGHTH AF•
JULY, 1943-JUNE, 1945

SouthEast *England* June, 1944
392nd Bomb Group

WENDLING

•LONDON

0 10 20
Miles

The graphics below illustrate changes in call-letters that affected the 392nd Bomb Group. The top configuration represents the original use of bar codes to identify squadrons assignments as issued in August, 1943. The bottom row depicts the revised squadron codes as mandated by the 2nd Bombardment Division directive regarding group tail markings in May, 1944. Note the addition of the plus sign.

576ᵀᴴBS • 577ᵀᴴBS • 578ᵀᴴBS • 579ᵀᴴBS

By midsummer 1944, most of the groups B-24's were displaying the last three digits from the tail serial number as an additional means of identification. Black or Identification Yellow paint was used depending upon aircraft surface finish. The two photo's above serve to illustrate the difference in both the size and placement of these three digits, and these are typical characteristic of the actual application of this system within the 392 Bomb Group.

The 392nd underwent a series of modifications to its' tactical marking schemes beginning almost from the moment they landed in the United Kingdom. The application of the various markings, while not the most inconsistent of the Eighth Air Force, were still rather flexible when taken as a whole. For example, the Circle 'D' tail marker could range in diameter from one aircraft to another by as much as four inches.

This crash site photo provides a glimpse of both the tail and wing tactical markings of the 392nd BG.

This tail shot affords a good close-up look at the groups first pattern tactical marking, call-letter and the SD110 squadron fuselage code.

A close look at the photo above revels the original aircraft identification number on the outward facing fin surface. Only the very tips of this original configuration is now visible, having been overpainted with the 36" horizontal black tail band. The aircraft call-letter in this case has been painted on with white rather than masked out to allow the natural metal under surface to show through.

1ST COMBAT BOMBARDMENT WING (H)

1ST BOMBARDMENT (AIR) DIVISION

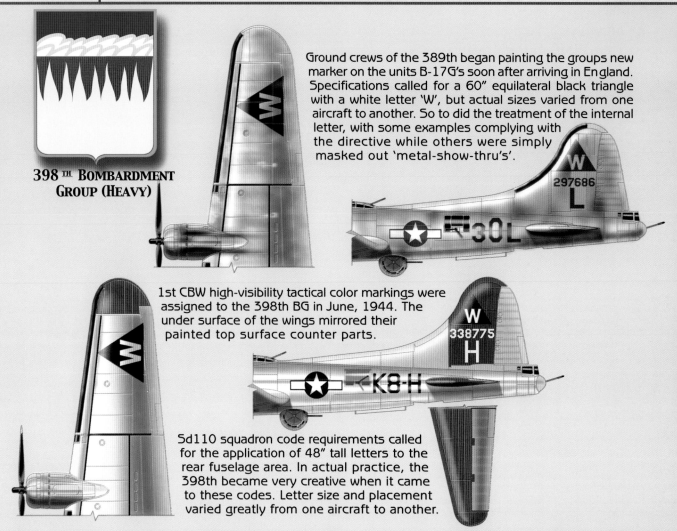

398TH BOMBARDMENT GROUP (HEAVY)

Ground crews of the 389th began painting the groups new marker on the units B-17G's soon after arriving in England. Specifications called for a 60" equilateral black triangle with a white letter 'W', but actual sizes varied from one aircraft to another. So to did the treatment of the internal letter, with some examples complying with the directive while others were simply masked out 'metal-show-thru's'.

297686
R-30L

1st CBW high-visibility tactical color markings were assigned to the 398th BG in June, 1944. The under surface of the wings mirrored their painted top surface counter parts.

338775
K8-H

Sd110 squadron code requirements called for the application of 48" tall letters to the rear fuselage area. In actual practice, the 398th became very creative when it came to these codes. Letter size and placement varied greatly from one aircraft to another.

N8
600TH BMB SQDN

3O
601ST BMB SQDN

K8
602ND BMB SQDN

N7
603RD BMB SQDN

•398TH BOMBARDMENT GROUP (HEAVY)•
'HELL FROM HEAVEN'
•STATION NO.131•
NUTHAMPSTEAD A/F-HERTFORDSHIRE
•CAMPAIGNS•
AMERICAN THEATER
AIR OFFENSIVE-EUROPE • NORMANDY
NORTHERN FRANCE • RHINELAND
ARDENNES-ALSACE • CENTRAL EUROPE
•ASSIGNED EIGHTH AF•
APRIL,1944-MAY,1945

This photograph, unusual for its' positioning of the crew mid-fuselage as opposed to the nose area, affords a good look at the vertically elongated '0' of this aircraft's 601st Bomb Squadron code. This Big '0' almost constituted a signature piece for this unit.

Although the photo above leaves a lot to be desired as far as clarity and lighting uniformity are concerned, it does provide a look at an unusual 398th Bomb Group tail marker application. The mid-tail section has been painted red in compliance with the 1st CBW directive. A somewhat smaller white triangle appears to have been painted over the existing group marker, leaving a thin black border around the newer image. A black 'W' has than been painted onto the inner white triangle.

A distinguishing feature of 398th Bomb Group aircraft centers around the placement of their fuselage SD110 squadron codes and call-letters. Most notable among these differentiative characteristics was the use of the 'zero' numeral by the 601st Bomb Squadron. As the lower example on the facing page illustrates, a vertically elongated '0' sandwiched between the first letter of the squadron code and the call-letter was a typical configuration for 601st aircraft. The 600th and 603rd Bomb Squadrons on the other hand chose to separate the call-letter from the SD110 code, while the 602nd preferred a grouping similar to that of the 601st, inserting however, a hyphen between the squadron code and call-letter. A close look at the photograph to the immediate right provides a sample of the different fuselage code applications among 398th Bomb Group squadrons. The aircraft in the immediate foreground shows the separation method employed by the 602nd BS. The aircraft immediately behind and slightly to the left of this aircraft

belongs to the 600th Bomb Squadron and shows the grouping method employed by that unit. On the left side of the aircraft, this grouping would be centerally located between the waist gunners window station and the rear horizontal stabilizers leading edge plane.

94TH **COMBAT BOMBARDMENT WING (H)**

1ST **BOMBARDMENT (AIR) DIVISION**

401ST BOMBARDMENT GROUP (HEAVY)

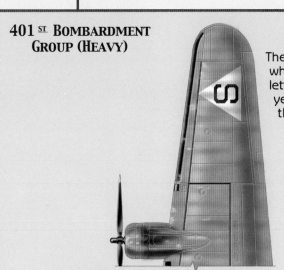

The 401st BG tail and wing tactical marker called for a white, 76" equilateral triangle with a 36" tall Insignia Blue letter 'S' contained therein. Additionally, a 24" yellow call-letter was applied just below the existing aircraft I.D. number.

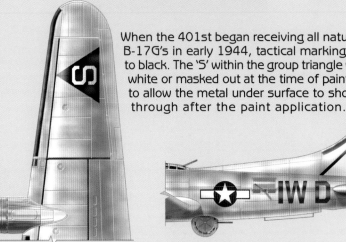

48" tall Sd110 squadron codes were applied to either side of the fuselage with Identification Yellow. Positioning of these codes varied among the squadrons.

When the 401st began receiving all natural metal finished B-17G's in early 1944, tactical markings were converted to black. The 'S' within the group triangle was either painted white or masked out at the time of painting to allow the metal under surface to show through after the paint application.

High-visibility tail markings began appearing on 401st B-17's by midsummer, 1944. The diagonally 48" wide yellow band was usually trimmed top and bottom with 3-4" wide black bands. The markings on many existing group aircraft were simply masked out prior to the new stripe being sprayed on the tail surface. This accounts for the bare metal areas surrounding the call-letters and I.D. numbers in so many war time photo's.

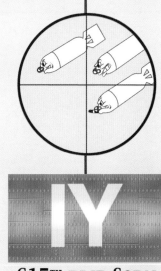

SC

IN

IW

IY

612TH **BMB SQDN**

613TH **BMB SQDN**

614TH **BMB SQDN**

615TH **BMB SQDN**

•401ST BOMBARDMENT GROUP (HEAVY)•
'BOWMAN'S BOMBERS'
•STATION NO.128•
DEENETHORPE A/F-NORTHAMPTONSHIRE
•CAMPAIGNS•
AIR OFFENSIVE-EUROPE • NORMANDY
NORTHERN FRANCE • RHINELAND
ARDENNES-ALSACE • CENTRAL EUROPE
•ASSIGNED EIGHTH AF•
NOVEMBER, 1943-MAY, 1945

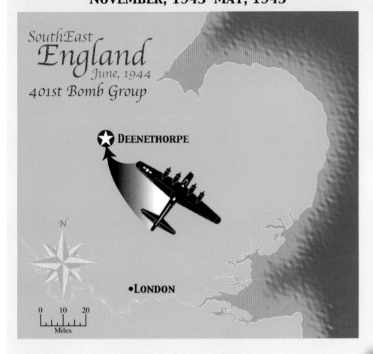

This is a view of a B-17's tactical tail markings through its severely flak damaged right vertical stabilizer. Although a some what sobering photo, it nevertheless does afford a close look at the geometric, angle edged stencil lettering. This was an almost universal feature within the Eighth Air Force.

As can be seen in these two first pattern marking photographs, the squadron codes were located above the rear wing area, forward the national insignia. The call-letters can be seen just forward the horizontal stabilizers. This was the standard positioning for right side fuselage applications in all squadrons of the 401st BG.

The image below is an excellent wartime photo of 'Maiden U.S.A.' s/n 44-6508 which served with the 401st BG from September 23, 1944 until it's return to the United States in June of 1945. This aircraft was heavily damaged by flak on it's thirty fifth combat mission over Berlin on 23Feb45. Having completed its' bomb run, 'Maiden U.S.A.' continued on an easterly heading with only two engines and landed at Kuflevo AF in the Soviet Union where the crew was interred and officially listed by the Army Air Force as 'Missing In Action' for seven weeks. Both ship and crew were ultimately released and returned to their unit.

This particular shot offers an excellent view of the starboard application of the squadron code and aircraft call-letter. Note the difference in placement of these elements compared to the port side application as depicted in the illustration on the facing page.

Temporarily grounded and awaiting a break in the weather, these B-17G's of the 615th Bomb Squadron display the proper left side fuselage positioning of their assigned SD110 code and call-letters. Both the 613th and 615th Bomb Squadrons applied this method of marking. The 612th and 614th Bomb Squadrons on the other hand, utilized this same method on the right side of the fuselage only. On the left side of the aircraft, the squadron code and call-letter were grouped together and positioned aft the waist gunners window.

445TH BOMBARDMENT GROUP (HEAVY)

Of special interest here is the stenciled numeral '3' on the no.4 outboard engine cowling. On the opposite wing there was a numeral '9' likewise stenciled to the no.1 outboard engine cowling. During the early stages of the 445th BG's deployment in England, these markings served as reference points (i.e. nine-o-clock, three-o-clock, etc.) for the top turret gunner when calling out the direction of attacking enemy fighters to the other gun crews.

First pattern group markings called for the application of a 69" white disk containing a 36" Insignia Blue letter 'H'. Yellow call-letters, 24" tall, were applied to both tail surfaces beginning March, 1944.

SD110 squadron markings were also introduced in March, 1944. These called for 48" tall letters to be applied with blue-grey paint. An additional fuselage call-letter was also applied with Identification Yellow in an assortment of letter sizes, the largest of which appears to have been approximately 36" in height.

High-visibility tail were adopted by the 445th BG beginning in April, 1944. The 36" wide white band incorporated recently revised 24" tall group call-letters. All codes were applied with black paint on the groups natural metal finished B-24's.

The size of the black SD110 fuselage codes were in the same 48" height as that of their camouflaged predecessors.

700TH BMB SQDN

701ST BMB SQDN

702ND BMB SQDN

703RD BMB SQDN

•445TH BOMBARDMENT GROUP (HEAVY)•
•STATION NO.124•
TIBENHAM A/F-NORFOLK
•CAMPAIGNS•
AIR OFFENSIVE-EUROPE • NORMANDY
NORTHERN FRANCE • RHINELAND
ARDENNES-ALSACE • CENTRAL EUROPE
•ASSIGNED EIGHTH AF•
NOVEMBER, 1943-MAY, 1945

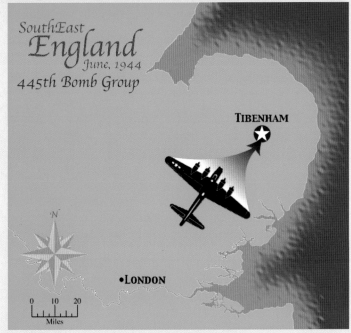

The original system of call-letters, while not the simplest by any means, was nevertheless workable. With the adoption of the new high-visibility tail markings however, the lid was removed from the proverbial can of worms. Someone within the 445th organization must have labored under the illusion that flight crews had too much time on their hands and consequently designed the following call-letter marking system to give the lads something to study and commit to memory while on those long, boring missions.

"Simplify, simplify": Whom ever it was that developed the call-letter marking system for the 445th Bomb Group was either unfamiliar with Thoreau's words of wisdom, or just missed his point altogether. Whereas most units strove to create simple and manageable means of individual aircraft recognition, the 445th went 180° in the opposite direction. The following graphics will hopefully assist in sorting-out this unnecessarily complex mechanism.

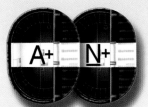

The 700th used 'A' thru 'M' with a plus sign. Letters 'N' thru 'Z' also used a plus sign *and* a bar symbol either above *or* below the call-letter.

700TH BOMB SQUADRON

The 701st employed 'A' thru 'M' with a plus sign *and* a bar symbol either above *or* below the letter. Letters 'N' thru 'Z' used a plus sign only.

701ST BOMB SQUADRON

The 702nd utilized the letters 'A' thru 'M' with a bar symbol either above *or* below the call-letter. 'N' thru 'Z' used no additional symbols

702ND BOMB SQUADRON

The 703rd used the letters 'A' thru 'M' with no additional symbols. 'N' thru 'Z' incorporated a bar symbol either above *or* below the call-letter.

703RD BOMB SQUADRON

The photo directly above is an excellent example of early 445th Bomb Group tactical markings. Note the course appearance of the national insignia which may well have been applied with a brush as a field update to the new AN-I-9a pattern. The remaining two photos provide good port and starboard views of the 445th's second pattern tactical markings. In contrast to the first example, the national insignia bears the clear, crisp look of a typical factory spray gun stencil application.

446TH BOMBARDMENT GROUP (HEAVY)

Shortly after their arrival in England, the upper right wing surface of the 446th BG's B-24's began to be painted with their new tactical marker. This consisted of a 48" high Insignia Blue 'H' centered on a 78" diameter Insignia White disc.

Tail sections received a 69" diameter white disk with a 36" tall letter. The 24" yellow call-letters were added to the tail sections in December, 1943. New SD110 squadron codes began showing up on 446th fuselages in March 1944. These were applied as 48" tall blue-grey letters.

Engine cowlings began to receive paint in their respective squadron colors, June '44.

With receipt of natural finished aircraft, squadron codes were applied in black while the wing marker became a black letter on a white disc.

446th BG 'Pathfinder' tail marking (mid 1944-'45)

High-visibility tactical tail markings were adopted by the 446th in May, 1944. The 36" wide black band carried a 24" yellow call-letter. These codes bore no bar symbols as this method of identification had been recently discontinued by the group.

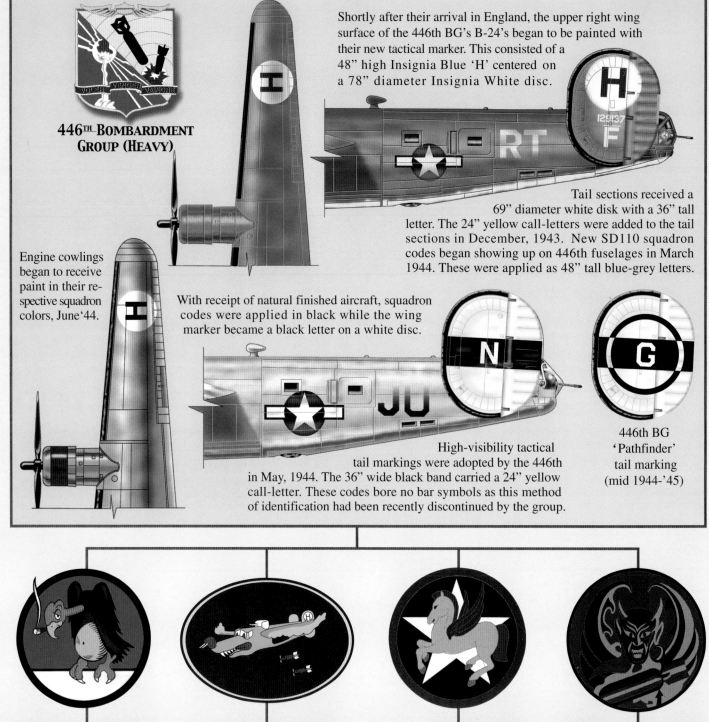

704TH BMB SQDN

705TH BMB SQDN

706TH BMB SQDN

707TH BMB SQDN

•446TH BOMBARDMENT GROUP (HEAVY)•
'FLY, AVENGE, VANQUISH'
STATION NO.125
FLIXTON AIRFIELD • SUFFOLK
•CAMPAIGNS•
AIR OFFENSIVE-EUROPE • NORMANDY
NORTHERN FRANCE • RHINELAND
ARDENNES-ALSACE • CENTRAL EUROPE
•ASSIGNED EIGHTH AF•
NOVEMBER, 1943-JULY, 1945

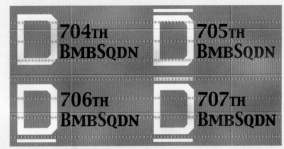

704TH BMBSQDN 705TH BMBSQDN
706TH BMBSQDN 707TH BMBSQDN

Early squadron identification bars were thin by normal standards with a maximum height of approximately 2".

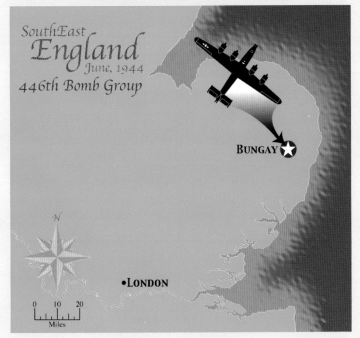

It is an unfortunate fact that most close-up tail shots of WWII aircraft involved crash sites or mishaps. In this example, note the unusually thin squadron indicator bar directly above the aircraft's call-letter 'E'.

Final elements of the 446th reached England in November, 1943 and began operations almost immediately. The 'Circle H' group marker was carried until the introduction of high-visibility tail markings in May, 1944. At the same time the secondary engine cowlings were ordered painted with the appropriate squadron colors (refer to previous page), and the 48" tall sky gray call-letters located on the aft section of each side of the fuselage were subsequently painted black on the newer all metal replacement aircraft.

This mission photo of a 705th Bomb Squadron aircraft contains all the typical tactical elements indicitive of the 446th Bomb Group.

Although the lighting could have been just a tad better, this is nevertheless a classic starboard view which displays all the elements of a first pattern 446th Bomb Group B-24 of the 707th Bomb Squadron. An excellent shot of the right wing marker application

The second pattern group markings in this photo show the lead aircraft to be a PPF [Pathfinder] of the 704th Bomb Squadron, while the aircraft trailing directly to the top left carries the 'JU' code of the 707th Bomb Squadron.

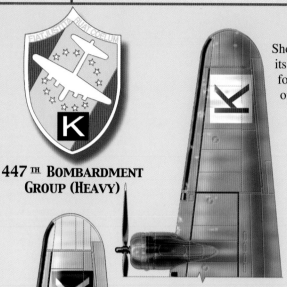

447TH BOMBARDMENT GROUP (HEAVY)

Shortly after their arrival at Rattlesden, the 447th was assigned its' group marker. On the upper right wing, specification called for a 48" tall Insignia Blue letter 'K' centered on a 72" X 57" Insignia White rectangle.

Specifications for tail applications called for a 48" Insignia Blue 'K' on a somewhat smaller 48" X 48" Insignia White square. Individual 24" tall call-letters were applied in Identification Yellow. Although SD110 squadron codes had been assigned to the group at the time of its' deployment, no identifying squadron codes were immediately affixed to 447th aircraft.

In late 1944 the 447th began displaying the Insignia Blue wing chevron of the 4th CBW. Further high-visibility color tactical markings were adopted in February, 1945. This included the application of Identification Yellow to tail and wing surfaces. Existing 4th CBW wing chevrons were generally not removed from existing applications.

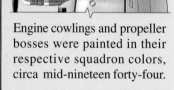

Engine cowlings and propeller bosses were painted in their respective squadron colors, circa mid-nineteen forty-four.

The new specifications included two medium green stripes that encircled the entire rear fuselage.

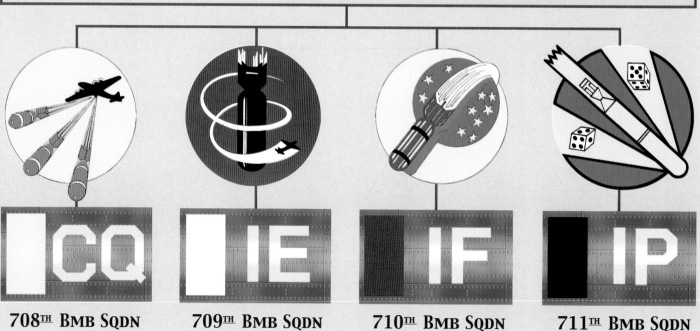

708TH BMB SQDN   **709TH BMB SQDN**   **710TH BMB SQDN**   **711TH BMB SQDN**

•447TH BOMBARDMENT GROUP (HEAVY)•
'LET JUSTICE BE DONE, LET THE HEAVENS FALL'
STATION NO.126
RATTLESDEN AIRFIELD • SUFFOLK
•CAMPAIGNS•
AIR OFFENSIVE-EUROPE • NORMANDY
NORTHERN FRANCE • RHINELAND
ARDENNES-ALSACE • CENTRAL EUROPE
•ASSIGNED EIGHTH AF•
NOVEMBER, 1943-AUGUST, 1945

The flak damaged tail section of 'A Bit 'O Lace' affords a close-up view of the 'Square K' emblem and aircraft identification numbers with small unfilled stencil lines. Note the unpainted metal replacement rudder, soon to be replaced once again.

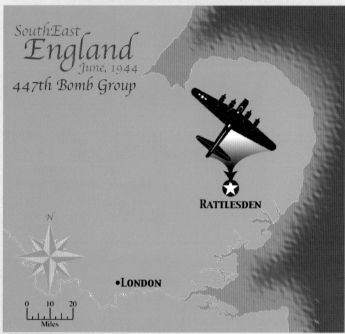

Entered combat December, 1943 with dual color camouflaged aircraft which, for security reasons, displayed no squadron markings for the first several months of their tour. In early 1944 the first unpainted B-17's began to arrive and with them numerous changes to the group's marking profile. The propeller bosses of all aircraft were directed to be painted in squadron colors and later the engine cowling rings received the same treatment. A group identification device was introduced in December of 1944 which consisted of an Insignia Blue chevron applied to the top right and bottom left outer wing surface areas. This means of unit identification

The middel photo shows Bit 'O Lace all patched-up and back in service. This early 1945 rare color image shows a typical high-visibility tactical marking scheme for the 447th Bomb Group. The lower photo shows just how effective these markings were within an Eighth AAF squadron/group formation during WWII.

was replaced by yet another change in February, 1945. This directive called for the painting of the entire rear vertical stabilizer assembly in Identification Yellow. Additionally the top surface area of both rear vertical stabilizers were to receive the same treatment as were the outer tips of the main wings. Finally the application of two vertical stripes, each measuring 24" with a 12" gap between, was directed to be painted circumfluent the aft fuselage area just slightly forward of the rear horizontal stabilizer. Fortunately for the ground maintenance crews, this latter directive did not mandate the removal of the recently applied chevrons from the wings,

This final image gives a good representation of the size relationship and placement of the 447th Bomb Group's second pattern, high-visibility tail/fuselage marking scheme.

448TH BOMBARMENT GROUP (HEAVY)

When the 448th first arrived in England the only tactical unit marking was a 12" white letter stenciled to the bottom of each vertical tail fin. Numbers 2,3,4 & 5 represented the 712th, 713th, 714th & 175th Sqdns respectively. The Circle ' I ' began to appear on 448th B-24's in December, 1944. The wing carried a 78" blue letter.

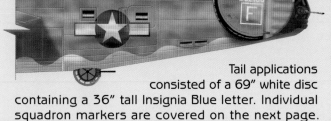

Tail applications consisted of a 69" white disc containing a 36" tall Insignia Blue letter. Individual squadron markers are covered on the next page.

448th squadrons began to display code letters on fuselages in March '44. These were 48" tall letter combinations, blue-grey on camouflaged, black on metal finished aircraft. The Circle ' I ' disc continued to be displayed on the right wings.

High-visibility tails were adopted in May 1944. The 36" diagonal black displayed the geometric squadron markers and individual aircraft call-letters, both in yellow. The symbols averaged 26" in height while the call-letters measured approximately 22".

712TH BMB SQDN

713TH BMB SQDN

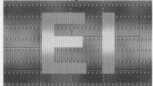

714TH BMB SQDN

715TH BMB SQDN

•448TH BOMBARDMENT GROUP (HEAVY)•
'DESTROY'
•STATION NO.146•
SEETHING A/F-NORFOLK
•CAMPAIGNS•
AIR OFFENSIVE-EUROPE • NORMANDY
NORTHERN FRANCE • RHINELAND
ARDENNES-ALSACE • CENTRAL EUROPE
•ASSIGNED EIGHTH AF•
DECEMBER, 1943-JUNE, 1945

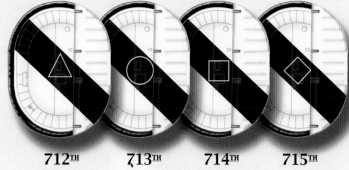

712TH   713TH   714TH   715TH

A direct carry-over from the 448th Bomb Groups' early attempts at squadron identification and aircraft call-letter recognition was the use of the aforementioned geometric symbols. These symbols varied in both line weight (although specifications called for a two-inch line width) and in the case of the triangle, shape as well. These inconsistencies however were minor and the important fact remains that these symbols were in fact a constant within the 448th Bomb Group framework. The graphic images displayed at the top of this text column depicts these geometric squadron symbols as applied with a somewhat narrower line width than the standard two inch width. The photograph at left provides a good close-up look at a starboard fin application of a 712th Bomb Squadron B-24. Of special interest in this particular photo is the application of a rather large duplicate call-letter 'N' to the inside surface of the port side fin. As previously mentioned, a standard application would have called for a duplicate image of that appearing on the outside surface, including the geometric symbol. This photograph however can be accurately dated as having been shot mid-to-late 1944, as it was during this period that the inclusion of the geometric symbol on the inside fin was discontinued.

As was the case with most bombardment groups within the Eighth Air Force structure, there were numerous modifications and variables that effected the 448th's tactical markings. However, with the exception of the groups initial attempts at squadron identification immediately following their arrival in England, the one constant was the utilization of geometric symbols as a means of individual squadron identification. When the group adopted their high-visibility tail marking pattern, the size of these squadron designating geometric shapes were, out of necessity, reduced in size to accommodate the limited diagonal band size. At this same time, a duplicate set of these symbols joined the previously relocated aircraft serial numbers on the inside facing surfaces of both tail fins. The sizes varied from between 24 and 36 inches in height and were applied with black paint on metal surfaces and with yellow on camouflaged ships.

Two wartime photographs which give a good look at both the first and second pattern application of the 448th Bomb Group tactical marking symtems. Note that in the upper photo the SD110 squadron codes are absent from the rear fuselage area. In the final months of 1944 the use of these codes had been ordered discontinued and subsequently these images were removed from most of the groups existing aircraft.

452ND BOMBARDMENT GROUP (HEAVY)

Labor Ad Futurum

Immediately after deployment to Great Britain the ground crews of the 452nd BG began applying the groups marker. Although shapes varied considerably, specifications called for a black letter 'L' on a white rectangular background. No SD110 squadron codes were adopted by the group during normal combat operations. It was only at wars end that 'anti-buzzing' codes were assigned, however no such codes were displayed prior to that time. Instead a 'plus/minus' (or 'bar') symbol system was incorporated with the tail call-letter.

As originally applied, tail call-letters appeared as a 20" tall Identification Yellow letter with (or without), the approiate plus/minus symbol.

The 45th Combat Bomb Wing high-visibility wing marking pattern as it applied to the 452nd BG was two parallel bands of Identification Yellow, each measuring 36", with a 60" separation between. The Square 'L' marker was removed to make room for the new marking device.

The high-visibility tail similarly consisted of two bands of Insignia Yellow paint as shown. The bottom band measured between 36" and 48" in height, the top band approximately 36". As with the wing application, there was roughly a 60" separation between the two bands.

728TH BMB SQDN   **729TH BMB SQDN**   **730TH BMB SQDN**   **731ST BMB SQDN**

•452ND BOMBARDMENT GROUP (HEAVY)•
'WORK FOR THE FUTURE
•STATION NO.142•
DEOPHAM A/F-NORFOLK
•CAMPAIGNS•
AIR OFFENSIVE-EUROPE • NORMANDY
NORTHERN FRANCE • RHINELAND
ARDENNES-ALSACE • CENTRAL EUROPE
•ASSIGNED EIGHTH AF•
JANUARY, 1944-JUNE, 1945

This wartime aerial photograph offers what appears to be a properly applied group marker to the upper right wing surface.

The composite image below represents a 'typical' application of a 452nd Bomb Groups tactical marking scheme as it would have appeared on all natural metal finished aircraft. The 452nd began receiving such ships in March, 1944 and it was in fact not until January of 1945 that the group adopted high-visibility tail markings. As such, these images are a far greater representation of what one would have seen in the air over south eastern England and Western Europe during the course of WWII.

As was the case with numerous other units within the Eighth Air Force during the war years, there existed a great deal of deviation in form when it came to the application of the groups Square 'L' marker. The original group marker was a white rectangle measuring sixty inches in height by forty inches in width on the rear vertical stabilizer. The devise for the upper surface of the right wing was to measure seventy-two by fifty-seven inches. Both devices were to incorporate a forty-eight inch tall uppercase letter 'L' applied with black, rather than Insignia Blue, paint. These requirements seem straight forward enough, however, for reasons unclear today, the specifications were only loosely adhered too. On some aircraft it appeared as if there was some confusion concerning the 'width vs. height, span vs. chord' layout requirements, with the result that stencils were apparently cut for tail applications applying the greatest measure to the width rather than the height. The result were 452nd markers that well overlapped onto the rudder area. Continuity aside, this was something that experienced ground crews tried to avoid whenever possible. Due to the frequency with which rudders on combat bombers were replaced due to battle damage, it made for an odd looking marker when a part of the original image went missing when the replacement component was fitted. In addition to this anomaly, the 452nd BG's 'square' marker seemed at times to have taken on a life of its' own, manifesting itself into a myriad of various shapes and sizes, seemingly at will.

2ND
COMBAT
BOMBARDMENT
WING (H)

2ND
BOMBARDMENT
(AIR) DIVISION

453RD BOMBARDMENT GROUP (HEAVY)

ATTACK AND DESTROY

The Circle 'J' marker was adopted by the 453rd in early 1944. White disc's measuring 69"(tail fin's) and 78" (upper right wing) were applied to the group's B-24's. Forty-eight inch blue-grey SD110 squadron codes began appearing on 453rd aircraft in late March of the same year.

Concurrent with the adoption of the groups' SD110 codes was the appearance of a plus symbol (+) after the tail call-letters on aircraft of the 734 and 735th squadrons. The 732nd and 733rd squadrons adopted no additional call-letter symbols at this particular time.

To further facilitate in-flight recognition, the 453rd Bomb Grp. sporadically applied squadron colors to aircraft propeller bosses beginning the first part of 1944.

With the receipt of natural metal finished B-24's, the tactical marker and squadron codes were appropriately converted.

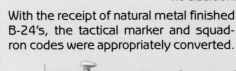

High-visibility tactical tail markings began to appear on 453rd aircraft in May, 1944. Two months later a revised tail call-letter system was adopted. By the end of 1944 the groups fuselage letter codes had been eliminated.

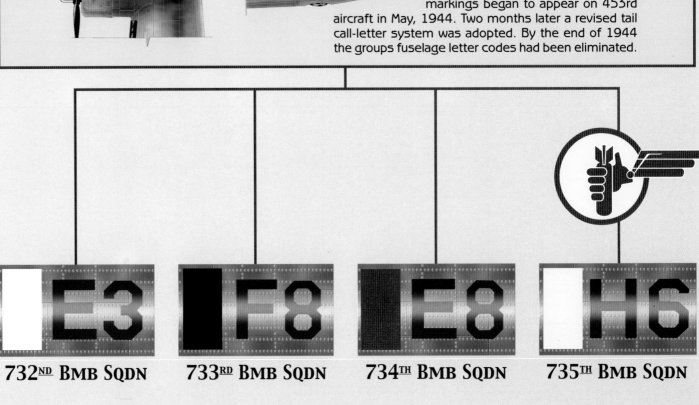

732ND BMB SQDN   **733RD BMB SQDN**   **734TH BMB SQDN**   **735TH BMB SQDN**

•453RD BOMBARDMENT GROUP (HEAVY)•
'ATTACK AND DESTROY'
•STATION NO.144•
OLD BUCKENHAM A/F-NORFOLK
•CAMPAIGNS•
AIR OFFENSIVE-EUROPE • NORMANDY
NORTHERN FRANCE • RHINELAND
ARDENNES-ALSACE • CENTRAL EUROPE
•ASSIGNED EIGHTH AF•
DECEMBER, 1943-MAY, 1945

The images below represent the standardized use of 'plus-minus' codes adopted by the 453rd Bomb Group in July of 1944. As was the case with several other 2nd Air Division groups, the diagonal stripe of the 453rd's high-visibility tail marking made the placement of an additional call-letter symbol something of a problem. When studying period photographs of this unit, a wide variety of applications of these symbols becomes very apparent. These differences not only apply in the comparison of one ship to another, but to the different positioning of these same symbols from the port and starboard tails on the same aircraft. Although a minor matter, it is nevertheless an interesting feature in the study of this subject.

732ND BOMB SQUADRON

733RD BOMB SQUADRON

734TH BOMB SQUADRON

735TH BOMB SQUADRON

There were several variations among squadrons of the 453rd in the use of call-letters. At various times the use of bar codes was implemented and than dropped by the groups squadrons. The application of these bar symbols were apparently more a means of differentiating between ships within the same squadrons that bore identical call-letters. This method contrasted with the later use of employing 'plus-minus' symbols as a means of identifying an aircrafts' actual squadron assignment. The 735th Bomb Squadron was the first within the 453rd Bomb Group to universally adapt a symbol after its' aircraft call-letters as a means of unit identification. A small yellow plus sign was added to the right of each ships tail call-letter. This represented the first organized use of a call-letter symbol within the 453rd Bomb Group as a means of determining individual aircraft squadron assignment. By midsummer 1944 a new policy was adopted which standardized the use of 'plus-minus' symbols within all squadrons of the 453rd BG. This standard use of symbols would continue to be employed by the group for the remainder of its' European combat tour.

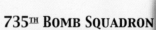

The photograph at the left displays the typical application of both the SD110 squadron code and the use of the call-letter symbol. The image directly above depicts a brief transition period which existed between the time the 453rd BG adopted high-visibility tail markings and the SD110 squadron codes.

457TH BOMBARDMENT GROUP (HEAVY)

FAIT ACCOMPLI

The Triangle 'U' tactical marker was applied to 457th B-17G's shortly after the groups arrival in England. 72" and 96" equilateral white triangles were applied to the tail and upper right wing respectively. Natural metal finish B-17's began to arrive shortly thereafter and these received a black triangle.

U 231383 F

Individual aircraft call-letters were assigned during this same period. Applications varied in size from between 36" and 48". Specifications called for the use of Identification Yellow but numerous white call-letters were in evidence for the first few months of deployment.

The 457th adopted the practice of painting propeller bosses in squadron colors in mid-1944. This applications would continue throughout the remainder of the war. Whether 5D110 squadron codes were ever assigned to the 457th is uncertain, what is certain is that no such codes were ever displayed by any of the groups squadron aircraft during the war.

U 48368 G

The 457th high-visibility tactical tail marking was adopted in the summer of 1944. This called for a 48" Insignia Blue stripe affixed to each side of the vertical tail surface at a prescribed 45° angle. The most common method of application employed a block-masking procedure which resulted in a metal or Olive Drab margin around any existing tail markings.

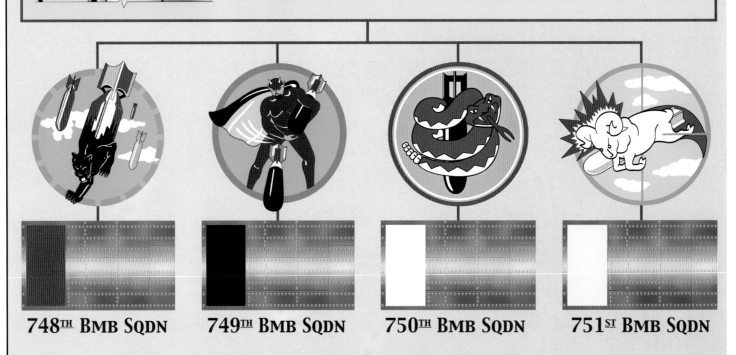

748TH BMB SQDN   **749TH BMB SQDN**   **750TH BMB SQDN**   **751ST BMB SQDN**

•457TH BOMBARDMENT GROUP (HEAVY)•
'AN ACCOMPLISHED FACT'
•STATION NO.130•
GLATTON A/F-HUNTINGDONSHIRE
•CAMPAIGNS•
AIR OFFENSIVE-EUROPE • NORMANDY
NORTHERN FRANCE • RHINELAND
ARDENNES-ALSACE • CENTRAL EUROPE
•ASSIGNED EIGHTH AF•
JANUARY, 1944-JUNE, 1945

This photo shows a typical aircraft identification method adopted by the 457th in the summer of 1944. The ships call-letter was combined with the last three digits of the tail I.D. number and applied to the nose in characters ranging from 12" to 18" in height. In the final months of the war some aircraft displayed an additional call-letter on either side of the chin turret.

This later example of a nose number application is clearly lacking missing the individual aircraft call-letter. Eliminating the call-letter from nose applications became standard practice within the 457th, although existing applications which contained this symbol were not ordered removed or repainted.

Upon initial deployment to England, 'The Fireball Outfit' as the 457th Bomb Group was popularly known, came equipped with the 'G' model B-17 painted in the standard factory applied two-color camouflage. In less than a month however the group began to receive unpainted natural metal finished aircraft. Both types of aircraft, painted and unpainted, were affixed with the groups tactical marker. As mentioned in the text on the previous page, it is not known specifically why the 457th never adopted the standard SD110 squadron codes. Whether the result of a clerical oversight or by design, the ground crews of the group were ultimately relieved of at least one additional duty when servicing their aircraft.

This photo affords a good detail look at a first pattern group tail marking scheme. The tactical markings on the tails of 457th ships, especially the call-letters, were of a diverse range of shapes and sizes with many applications clearly showing telltale signs of hand painting rather than that of a cleaner sprayed-on stencil application.

These three photographs show the evolution of tactical marking patterns within the 457th Bomb Group. Although not depicted here, there were some camouflaged B-17's which remained around to receive the groups high-visibility tactical tail marking.

458TH BOMBARDMENT GROUP (HEAVY)

Although all four squadrons displayed combat insignia, research has failed to disclose evidence that any such image ever existed for the group.

The 458ths' Circle 'K' first pattern tactical marker was applied to the groups B-24s almost the moment they touched English soil. Tail applications called for a 69" white disc containing a 36" blue letter therein. The wing bore a similar image, a 78" disc with the groups 48" Insignia Blue letter 'K'.

Application of the group marker necessitated the repositioning of the serial number to a point lower on the fin. A 24" call-letter was then added to the tail configuration. 5D110 squadron codes were applied in March 1944. These were blue-grey in color and averaged 51" in height. The white areas of the national insignia were muted to a neutral grey on many 458thBG aircraft in order to minimize this images inherent 'aiming point' characteristics.

Natural metal finished B-24s began arriving in April 1944. The groups first pattern markings were applied to these aircraft as either black and white images or, in some cases, black only with the metal under-surface showing through.

The 458ths' high-visibility tactical tail markings began appearing on the groups aircraft in May, 1944. Serial numbers were relocated to the inside top fin areas and a black red 24" call-letter was positioned within the newly applied 30" outward facing vertical white stripe.

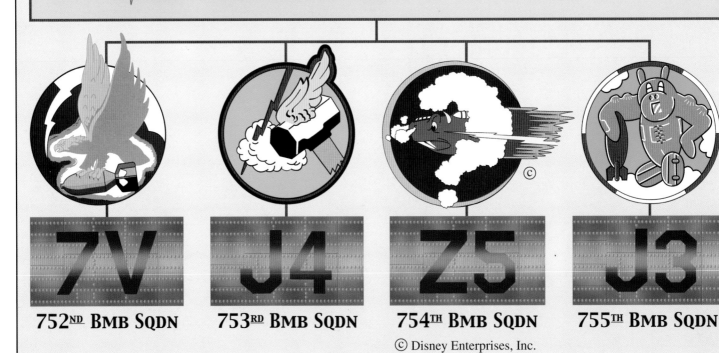

752ND BMB SQDN   753RD BMB SQDN   754TH BMB SQDN   755TH BMB SQDN

•458th Bombardment Group (Heavy)•
•Station No.123•
Horsham St Faith A/F-Norfolk
•Campaigns•
Air Offensive-Europe • Normandy
Northern France • Rhineland
Ardennes-Alsace • Central Europe
•Assigned Eighth AF•
January, 1944-June, 1945

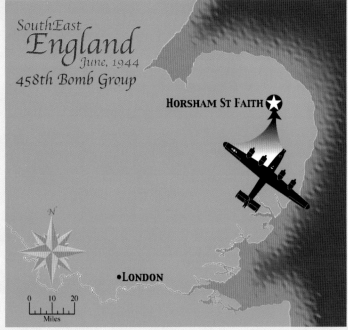

This image represents a proposed patch for a special unit formed within the 458th Bomb Group. The VB-1 AZON Guided Bomb project was the great-grand daddy of todays 'smart bombs' and was shrouded in secrecy until ultimately declassified in 1977. AZON, an synonym for 'azimuth only' was the invention of a Major Henry Rand and Mr. Thomas O'Donnell which allowed bombardiers a modem of decent control over 1,000 G.P. bombs after initial release from the aircraft. Radio controls coupled with extremely bright flares and smoke canisters attached to the tails assisted bombardiers in guiding the bombs to their designated targets. This patch was intended to be issued to aircrews assigned to the AZON Project, however the program was terminated before actual production of this piece began. Although never issued to the men who flew the missions, this is nonetheless an interesting piece of 458thBG history.

A typical application of 458th Bomb Group second pattern tactical markings. Although not shown in this particular photograph, 458th aircraft began adopting the use on 'nose numbers' very late in the war. These markings consisted of the last three digits of the aircrafts' serial number, followed by a hyphen, followed in turn by the call-letter. These were large letters and were applied with yellow paint on camouflaged ships and with black on natural metal finishes.

As was the case with numerous other groups assigned to the Eighth Army Air Force during this period of the war, each month brought with it either an addition or modification to the 458th Bomb Groups' tactical markings. Judging from the photographic evidence available today it would appear that the ground crews of the 458th were somewhat better prepared for these changes than some of their contemporaries in other groups. There is a consistency in all marking shapes and sizes among squadrons of the 458th that bespeaks a conscious, unified effort to maintain an expeditious method of applying everything from the SD110 fuselage codes to the groups' tail marking applications. This pattern of organized tactical marking application invariably helped ease the work load of the groups ground crews.

These two photographs depict the application of both first and second pattern 458th Bomb Group tactical markings to camouflaged aircraft, both belonging to the 752nd Bomb Squadron. Of special interest is what appears to be the numeral '9' which has been stenciled to the top outside surface of the number four engine cowling. The specific purpose of this symbol is unknown as it bears no apparent correlation to similar Eighth AAF applications.

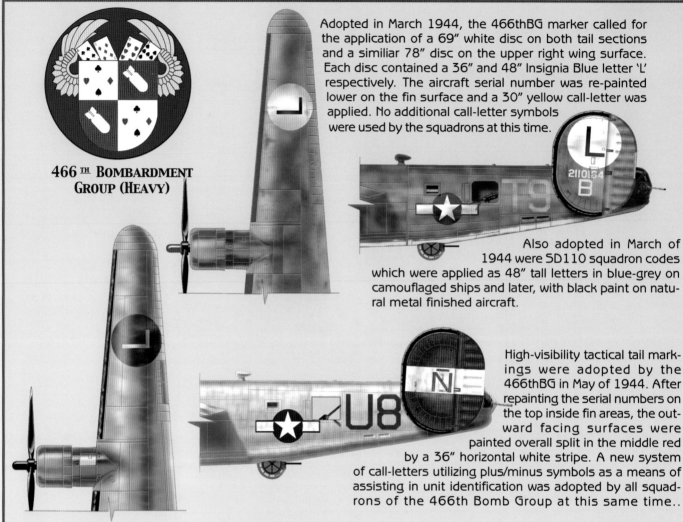

466TH BOMBARDMENT GROUP (HEAVY)

Adopted in March 1944, the 466thBG marker called for the application of a 69" white disc on both tail sections and a similiar 78" disc on the upper right wing surface. Each disc contained a 36" and 48" Insignia Blue letter 'L' respectively. The aircraft serial number was re-painted lower on the fin surface and a 30" yellow call-letter was applied. No additional call-letter symbols were used by the squadrons at this time.

Also adopted in March of 1944 were 5D110 squadron codes which were applied as 48" tall letters in blue-grey on camouflaged ships and later, with black paint on natural metal finished aircraft.

High-visibility tactical tail markings were adopted by the 466thBG in May of 1944. After repainting the serial numbers on the top inside fin areas, the outward facing surfaces were painted overall split in the middle red by a 36" horizontal white stripe. A new system of call-letters utilizing plus/minus symbols as a means of assisting in unit identification was adopted by all squadrons of the 466th Bomb Group at this same time..

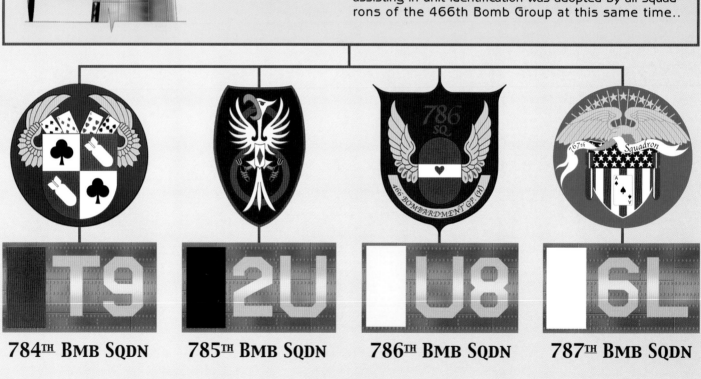

| 784TH BMB SQDN | 785TH BMB SQDN | 786TH BMB SQDN | 787TH BMB SQDN |

•466TH BOMBARDMENT GROUP (HEAVY)•
'THE FLYING DECK'
•STATION NO.120•
ATTLEBRIDGE A/F-NORFOLK
•CAMPAIGNS•
AIR OFFENSIVE-EUROPE • NORMANDY
NORTHERN FRANCE • RHINELAND
ARDENNES-ALSACE • CENTRAL EUROPE
•ASSIGNED EIGHTH AF•
MARCH, 1944-JUNE, 1945

CALL-LETTERS
In May of 1944 the following letter and plus/minus symbols were universally adopted by the 466th Bombardment Group.

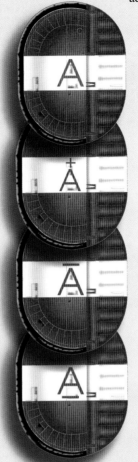

784TH BOMB SQUADRON

785TH BOMB SQUADRON

786TH BOMB SQUADRON

787TH BOMB SQUADRON

The use of assigned squadron colors on 466thBG engine cowlings was initiated in mid 1944 and universally adopted by all squadrons by early 1945. The question may arise as to why the second pattern illustration on the facing page does not carry the colors of the 786th Bomb Group on its' engine cowling ring. Battle damage forced this particular aircraft to crash land in Sweden on 21Jun44. This was prior to the adoption of the squadron color policy and consequently displays no such markings. Prior to this period, individual aircraft in all squadrons were known to employ the use of colors to the engine propeller bosses. These applications were random at best and no official policy regarding the use of assigned squadron colors were issued by 466th BG headquarters at this time.

UNIFORM SQUADRON COLOR APPLICATION/1945

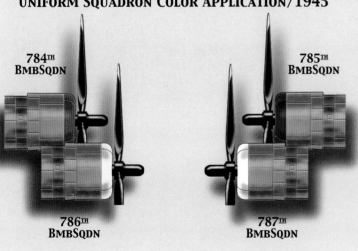

784TH BMBSQDN

785TH BMBSQDN

786TH BMBSQDN

787TH BMBSQDN

The upper and lower photographs are good representative images of both the first and second pattern tactical marking schemes for the 466thBG. Note the painted outer engine cowling rings in the bottom photo as well as the painted propeller bosses in the top photo.

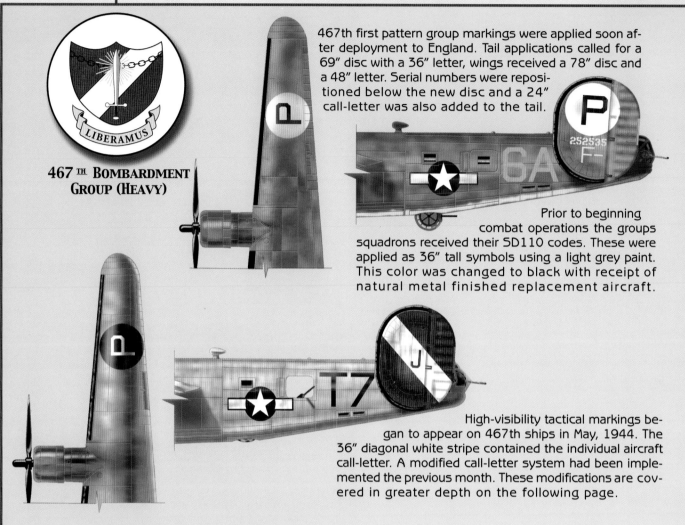

467TH BOMBARDMENT GROUP (HEAVY)

467th first pattern group markings were applied soon after deployment to England. Tail applications called for a 69" disc with a 36" letter, wings received a 78" disc and a 48" letter. Serial numbers were repositioned below the new disc and a 24" call-letter was also added to the tail.

Prior to beginning combat operations the groups squadrons received their SD110 codes. These were applied as 36" tall symbols using a light grey paint. This color was changed to black with receipt of natural metal finished replacement aircraft.

High-visibility tactical markings began to appear on 467th ships in May, 1944. The 36" diagonal white stripe contained the individual aircraft call-letter. A modified call-letter system had been implemented the previous month. These modifications are covered in greater depth on the following page.

788TH BMB SQDN   **789TH BMB SQDN**   **790TH BMB SQDN**   **791ST BMB SQDN**

•467TH BOMBARDMENT GROUP (HEAVY)•
'TO SET FREE'
•STATION No.145•
RACKHEATH A/F-NORFOLK
•CAMPAIGNS•
AMERICAN THEATER
AIR OFFENSIVE-EUROPE • NORMANDY
NORTHERN FRANCE • RHINELAND
ARDENNES-ALSACE • CENTRAL EUROPE
•ASSIGNED EIGHTH AF•
MARCH, 1944-JUNE, 1945

The 467th BG insignia doubles as a sign board for the base officers club. The Sword And Chain was situated at the end of the this typically English countryside pathway.

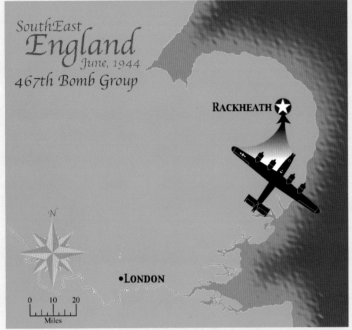

The images below were just about the only two that turned up while doing photographic research for the 467th that showed unobstructed close-ups of the nose numbers. The vast majority of front angle shots have crew members either partially or totally obscuring the individual tactical markings. This is quite natural as it probably didn't occur to anyone at the time that future generations would find such utilitarian objects a source of much interest. Be that as it may, in October 1944 the 467th adopted the policy of painting the

last three digits of the serial number on the aircrafts nose. These numbers ranged from 24" to 30" in height and were applied with white paint on camouflage and black paint on the groups all metal finished B-24s.

The Rackheath Aggies ground crews were kept busy after their arrival in Great Britain. In addition to everything else on their agenda, the paint was still wet from applying the first tactical marking schemes to the groups aircraft when everything they had just finished was ordered changed. Tail call-letters underwent a slight modification in April, just prior to the group being classified as operational. The images below illustrate these changes to the call-letters which were issued within one month of each other.

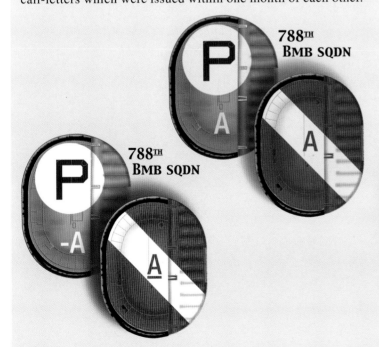

788TH BMB SQDN

788TH BMB SQDN

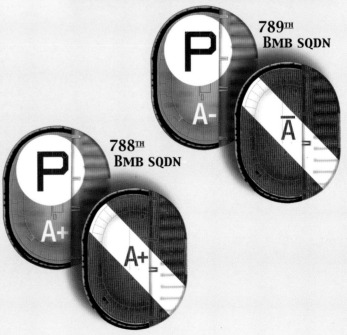

789TH BMB SQDN

788TH BMB SQDN

482ND BOMBARDMENT GROUP (PATHFINDER)
REDESIGNATED
482ND BOMBARDMENT GROUP (HEAVY)
NOVEMBER,1944

SD110 squadron codes were adopted by the 406th in October, 1943. These were 48" tall and positioned forward the national insignia. A 24" call-letter was applied to the tail section just below the aircraft serial number. There were no tactical markings affixed to the wings.

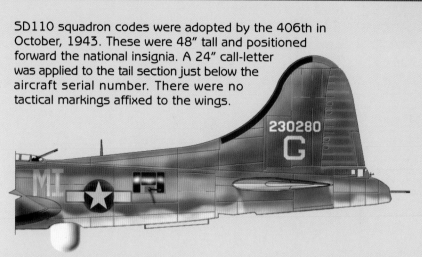

The initial B-24's assigned to the 814th Bomb Squadron displayed nothing more than the national insignia, all original insignia from previous unit assignments were hastily over painted. Later, no attempt was made to cover up the unit insignia of aircraft attached during training periods.

The 406th dispensed with displaying squadron codes on their aircraft for a period of several months until reinstated in September, 1944. By this time natural metal aircraft had arrived in the unit and all markings were applied with black paint. This time around the B-24's received SD110 squadron codes and these were applied aft the waist gunners window area.

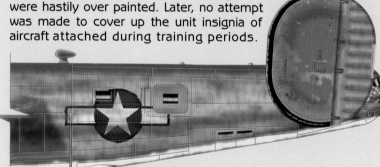

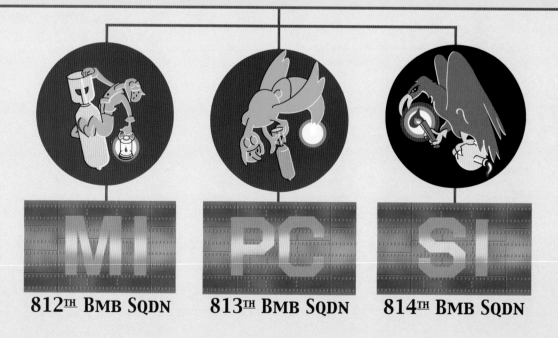

•482ND BOMBARDMENT GROUP (HEAVY)•
•STATION NO.102•
ALCONBURY A/F-HUNTINGDONSHIRE
•CAMPAIGNS•
AIR OFFENSIVE-EUROPE • NORMANDY
NORTHERN FRANCE • RHINELAND
ARDENNES-ALSACE • CENTRAL EUROPE
•ASSIGNED EIGHTH AF•
AUGUST, 1943-JUNE, 1945

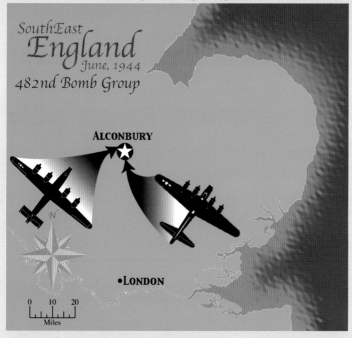

These two combat insignia belong to the same outfit, the 406th Bomb Squadron. This was a highly traveled unit that served in both the Pacific as well as in Europe.

Although the 406th was not permanently assigned to the 482nd Bomb Group, they were attached from early December 1943 until late February 1944. The 406th was presumably with the 482nd to learn the tricks-of -the-trade of airborne radar technology. These skills undoubtedly aided the 406th later on when they would participate in the Carpetbagger missions, a special operations effort which supplied resistance forces in Western Europe.

The top, or Disney, insignia was temporarily replaced by the lower image. The 406th did not however abandon their Indian Boy for long and in fact is today the current historical image for this unit. There have been two small modifications to this insignia over the years. Somewhere along the way the signal pistol in the belt and decorative border have been discarded from the original design.

By today's standards the 482nd Bomb Group would be categorized as a Spec Ops unit. The 482nd was activated in England and comprised of select VIII Bomber Command flight crews and key personnel from the 329th Bomb Squadron who had worked on the early Gee experiments. Ground crews were supplied from the 479th Antisubmarine Group when that unit was disbanded in November, 1943. The mission of this unit was essentially to develope and field test various improved airborne radar systems used in blind bombing, or BTO (Bombing Through Overcast). Early on the group would provide Pathfinder ships (PFF) to other Eighth Air Force bombing formations. After a time the 482nd became responsible for the training of specially designated air crews from the virtually every Bombardment group comprising the Eighth. These crews would learn the techniques of airborne radar operation and subsequently be returned to their original units to take up their new roll as designated group Pathfinders. This honor was not without it's risks however.

The life of a PFF crew was not an enviable one and carried with it not only much of the responsibility of a missions success or failure, but the increased dangers inherent with a radar equipped B-17 or B-24. This equipment was not only heavy and space consuming, it also required the addition on another crewman or 'Mickey' operator. The radome was a fully retractable unit which was located where the ball turret would normally be, thus reducing the Pathfinders defensive firepower. As if this wasn't enough, each PFF was required to carry a normal bomb load in addition to the smoke flares for marking the designated target area. In the Eighth Air Force, the prestige of being among the 'top bomber crews' came at a very high price.

Other than the assigned squadron codes, the only other tactical marking devise adopted by the 482nd Bomb Group was a 60" solid black equilateral triangle. This symbol began appearing on the group's B-17's in September of 1944, but for whatever reason, there is no evidence that it was ever affixed to the B-24's of the 814th Squadron.

92ND/4TH COMBAT BOMBARDMENT WINGS (H)

3RD BOMBARDMENT (AIR) DIVISION

486TH BOMBARDMENT GROUP (HEAVY)

The 486th was ordinarily very keen on the use of visuals within its' organizational structure. However, they appear to have failed to develop a combat insignia for the themselves.

The 486th originally went to war flying B-24's displaying the Square 'O' tactical marker. These measured 48" on the tail and 60" on wings. Both contained a 36" and 48" letter respectively. A 24" tall yellow call-letter was painted just below the serial number. An additional call-letter was applied to the fuselage area, forward the national insignia. The SD110 squadron code was located to the rear of the waist gunners window. Both of these measured 40" in height in a light-grey.

The call-letter was dropped from the tail and added forward the national insignia and applied in their respective squadron colors.

The 486ths' B-24's were replaced with B-17's in July, 1944. All aircraft received were all natural metal finished and received the groups newly assigned Square 'W' tactical marker. Specifications called for a 48" square on the tail with a 57" X 72" rectangle on the wings. In December '44, two converging 36º stripes were directed to be applied to the upper right and lower left wing surfaces. In early '45 a new high-visibility tactical color scheme was adopted by the 486th. Color applications included the entire tail surface as well as the tips of the wings and leading edges of the horizontal stabilizers. Three 24" color bands with 12" separations were added to the rear fuselage.

| 832ND BMB SQDN | 833RD BMB SQDN | 834TH BMB SQDN | 835TH BMB SQDN |

•486TH BOMBARDMENT GROUP (HEAVY)•
•STATION NO.174•
SUDBURY A/F-SUFFOLK
•CAMPAIGNS•
AIR OFFENSIVE-EUROPE • NORMANDY
NORTHERN FRANCE • RHINELAND
ARDENNES-ALSACE • CENTRAL EUROPE
•ASSIGNED EIGHTH AF•
MARCH, 1944-AUGUST, 1945

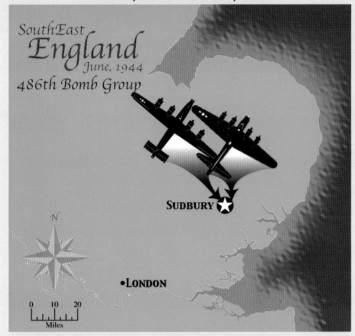

Although somewhat out of focus, the photo to the left is unusual in that the group tactical marker is that of a white square containing a black letter on a painted late war tail surface. Normal applications called for a white letter on a black square such as that in the top photo. An especially interesting detail in the latter item is the presence of armed Wehrmacht troops guarding the downed 486th aircraft. This shot is so unusual that it almost has the look of a still photo taken during the filming of a Hollywood war movie. It is a sobering reminder of the very real dangers faced by allied airmen in the skies over Western Europe.

From a visual perspective the 486th Bomb Group is one of the most interesting units within the Eighth Army Air Force. A name that should stand out among aficionados of WWII nose art is that of one Cpl. Philip Brinkman. Assigned to the 834th Bomb Squadron, Brinkman was a commercial illustrator in civilian life, and created for his squadron some of the most memorable art work to ever grace the sides of any aircraft, anywhere at any time. In addition the work he generated on other ships within the squadron, Brinkman in the process of working on the twelfth and final B-24

in his 'Zodiac' series when the group made the transition to B-17s. Nevertheless, the 'Scorpio' nose art he designed for B-24 #42-52762 (depicted at left) so impressed the squadron commander that this image was adopted as the official combat insignia of the 834th Bomb Squadron. For those unfamiliar with the nose art created by Phil Brinkman, it is well worth the effort to spent the time to get acquainted with this talented individuals work. An interesting historical footnote is the fact that during the forty-nine combat missions flown by the 486th Bomb Group in B-24's, not one of the eleven 'Zodiac's' painted by Brinkman ever failed to return to base. Maybe the German gunners appreciated good art.

Very shortly after making the transition from B-24's, the 486th Bomb Group adopted the Square 'W' tactical marking. The groups former Square 'O' marker was dropped because there was some concern that with the groups conversion to B-17's their old marker might be to easily confused with the Square 'D' tactical marker belonging to the 100th Bomb Group. When the 4th Combat Bomb Wing chevron was ordered applied to the upper right wing surface of the groups aircraft, existing Square 'W' markers were either removed or simply painted over and omitted from replacement aircraft wing applications. The photo below illustrates a typical first pattern Square 'W' tail marking scheme. Note the SD110 squadron code on the rear fuselage. Use of these codes would be dropped when the 486th Bomb Group adopted their new high-visibility tactical marking theme during the end of January, 1945.

Also in January '45, the 486th BG adopted the use of 24" wide bands of color applied to the nose sections of all their B-17's.

832ND BOMB SQUADRON

834TH BOMB SQUADRON

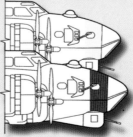

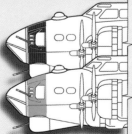

833RD BOMB SQUADRON

835TH BOMB SQUADRON

487TH BOMBARDMENT GROUP (HEAVY)

GENTLEMEN FROM HELL

Originally deployed with B-24's the 487th adopted the Square 'P' as their group marking device. Applications for the tail specified a 48" white square while tail applications called for a slightly different 72" X 57" rectangle. Both images were to contain a 36" Insignia Blue letter. Individual call-letters were applied in 24" yellow characters below the serial number.

Squadron codes plus an additional call-letter were applied to the fuselage as 48" tall characters in a light-grey paint.

Along with the new aircraft came new high-visibility tactical markings. The entire tail surface of the newly assigned B-17's were painted Identification Yellow. The Square 'P' marker was retained but was converted to a white-on-black image. Additionally, the entire leading surface areas of both horizontal stabilizers recieved an application of yellow paint, top and bottom. This also included painting the tips of the wings.

In December of 1944 the 487th began applying the 4th Combat Bomb Wing chevron to the upper right and lower left wing surfaces Each yellow and blue band measured approximately 48" in overall width.

836TH BMB SQDN

837TH BMB SQDN

838TH BMB SQDN

839TH BMB SQDN

•487th Bombardment Group (Heavy)•
the 'Gentlemen From Hell'
•Station No.137•
Lavenhan A/F-Suffolk
•Campaigns•
Air Offensive-Europe • Normandy
Northern France • Rhineland
Ardennes-Alsace • Central Europe
•Assigned Eighth AF•
April, 1944-June, 1945

Although this is an excellent operational shot of a 487th Bomb Group B-17, the yellow tail and wing markings are barely discernible in a black-and-white image format.

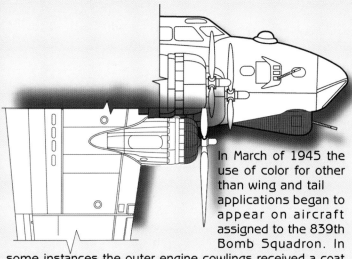

The 487th originally entered combat as a B-24 outfit but after less that three months into their operations, the group began to make the transition to the B-17. This transition was completed in August of 1944 when the group had effectively phased the '24's out of their combat operations.

The original inventory of B-24's assigned to the 487th were of the typical two color camouflage type, but replacement aircraft displaying natural metal finishes began arriving as early as May 1944. It was not long after this that the group began adding the first B-17 to their inventory. All these aircraft were of the 'G' series and also featured natural metal finishes. To date no camouflaged 'Forts' are known to have ever been assigned to the 487th Bomb Group.

The B-17's originally had the groups tactical marker affixed to the upper right wing surface area. This image was white-on-black and generally measured 57" square. These symbols were removed however the following December to make room for the new 4th Combat Bomb Wing chevron. The images to the right illustrate typical first pattern 487th Bomb Group markings as they were applied to the units B-17's.

In March of 1945 the use of color for other than wing and tail applications began to appear on aircraft assigned to the 839th Bomb Squadron. In some instances the outer engine cowlings received a coat of Insignia Red paint while other ships within the same squadron opted to apply this same color to the entire chin turret area. Reportedly, the 837th Squadron began painting the engine cowlings of their aircraft with Identification Yellow during this same time period. Neither of these colors however were ever officially adopted within the 487th Bomb Group.

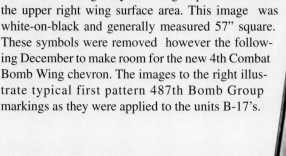

489ᵀᴴ BOMBARDMENT GROUP (HEAVY)

EX TENEBRIS LUX VERITATIS

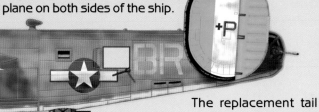

The Circle 'W' configuration on the right wing was originally intended to be displayed on tail surfaces as well. For reasons discussed later, only the wing application remained intact. This was a white disc that varied in size from between 78" and 84" in diameter. 5D110 squadron codes were applied as 48" tall characters using a light-grey paint. These were located aft the waist gunners window and forward the tail plane on both sides of the ship.

The replacement tail design consisted of an overall coat of a light grass-green paint divided vertically by a 30" white stripe. Individual aircraft call-letters measuring 24" in height were applied to this stripe utilizing black paint. Within the squadrons the 844th used letters only; the 845th used a minus sign under the letter; the 846th a plus sign before the letter and the 847th a minus sign after the letter.

With reciept of all metal finished aircraft the wing marker became a white on black image. The 5D110 codes, while remaining in the same location, were applied in black paint.

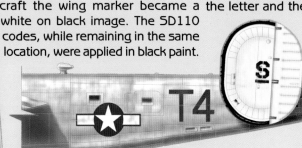

Upon their transfer from the 95th to the 20th Combat Bomb Wing, the 489th Bomb Group adopted an all yellow tail in keeping with the 20th CBW's high-visibility tactical tail marking policy. Unlike the other groups already assigned to the 20th, the 489th did not employ the use of a black stripe on its' tail applications.

844ᵀᴴ BMB SQDN

845ᵀᴴ BMB SQDN

846ᵀᴴ BMB SQDN

847ᵀᴴ BMB SQDN

•489th Bombardment Group (Heavy)•
'Removing The Darkness With The Light Of Truth'
•Station No.365•
Halesworth A/F-Suffolk
•Campaigns•
American Theater
Air Offensive-Europe • Normandy
Northern France • Rhineland
•Assigned Eighth AF•
May, 1944-November, 1944

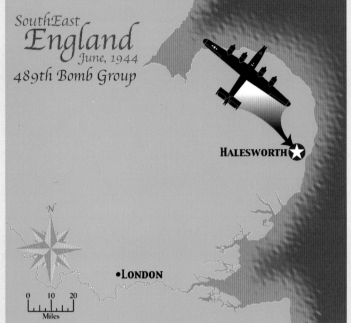

Due in large part undoubtedly to the fact that the 489th Bomb Groups assignment to the Eighth Air Force lasted less than eight months, the availability of photographic source material is somewhat on the thin side. Towards the end of 1944 it was determined that the air war in Europe was well in hand and it was consequently decided to redeploy the 489th to the Pacific Theater of Operations. Thus it was that the group was transferred back to the United States for additional training in B-29's in preparation for doing battle against Japan, a deployment which as it turned out, never took place. The photograph above shows the second pattern 95th Combat Bomb Wing tail application of the 489th Bomb Group. This was the design that superceded the previously discussed Circle 'W' motif.

Upon arrival at their new base at Halesworth, the ground crews of the 489th Bomb Group set about the task of applying the newly assigned tactical markings to the groups inventory of B-24's. Original specifications pertaining to the 489th called for, among other things, the application to the outside surface areas of both tail fins of a white disc measuring approximately 70 inches in diameter. Contained therein would be a 36 inch uppercase 'W', rendered in black as opposed to Insignia Blue. Concurrently, a similar configuration was directed to be applied to the upper right wing surface area. The directive pertaining to this devise likewise called for a white disc, in this case measuring approximately 80 inches in diameter and containing a 48 inch black uppercase 'W'. Work on this project came to an abrupt about face when headquarters received word that they were to be issued a new tail identification system. Ground crews were apprised

 that the wing application would remain the same but they were ordered to remove any recently applied Circle 'W' markers from all tail sections. Not having anything much better to do with their time, the ground personnel undoubtedly went about complying with this new change-order with unbridled enthusiasm. At any rate, the image at left depicts these early efforts and is representative of what the groups tails

This overhead aerial shot provides a good look at the wing application of the Circle 'W' marker of the 489th Bomb Group. As previously stated, even though this symbol was dropped from 489th tail applications, it continued to be displayed on the upper right wings.

93RD **COMBAT BOMBARDMENT WING (H)**

3RD **BOMBARDMENT (AIR) DIVISION**

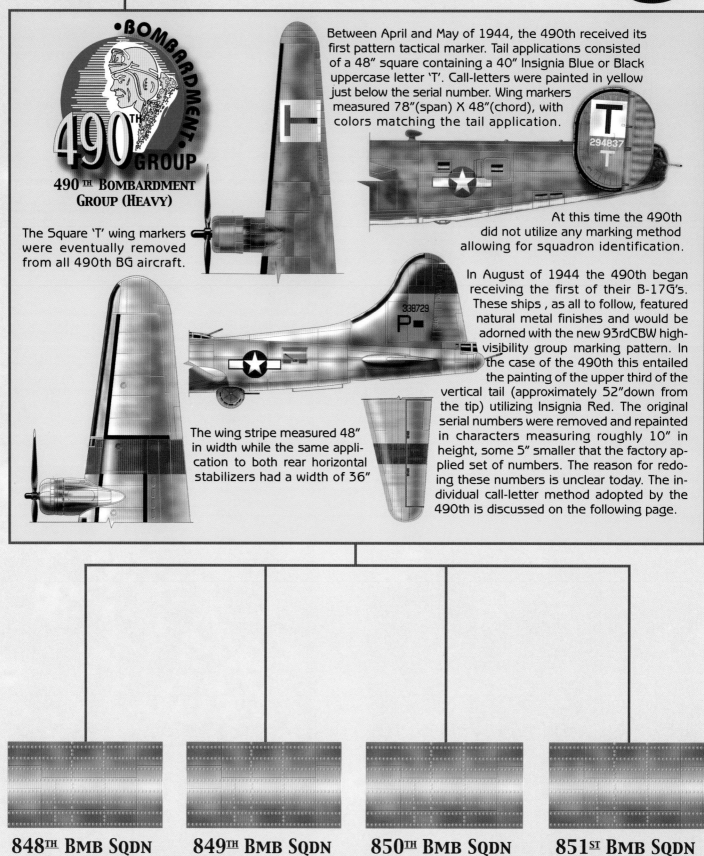

·BOMBARDMENT·

490TH **GROUP**

490TH **BOMBARDMENT GROUP (HEAVY)**

The Square 'T' wing markers were eventually removed from all 490th BG aircraft.

Between April and May of 1944, the 490th received its first pattern tactical marker. Tail applications consisted of a 48" square containing a 40" Insignia Blue or Black uppercase letter 'T'. Call-letters were painted in yellow just below the serial number. Wing markers measured 78"(span) X 48"(chord), with colors matching the tail application.

294837

At this time the 490th did not utilize any marking method allowing for squadron identification.

338729

P■

In August of 1944 the 490th began receiving the first of their B-17G's. These ships, as all to follow, featured natural metal finishes and would be adorned with the new 93rdCBW high-visibility group marking pattern. In the case of the 490th this entailed the painting of the upper third of the vertical tail (approximately 52"down from the tip) utilizing Insignia Red. The original serial numbers were removed and repainted in characters measuring roughly 10" in height, some 5" smaller that the factory applied set of numbers. The reason for redoing these numbers is unclear today. The individual call-letter method adopted by the 490th is discussed on the following page.

The wing stripe measured 48" in width while the same application to both rear horizontal stabilizers had a width of 36"

848TH **BMB SQDN**

849TH **BMB SQDN**

850TH **BMB SQDN**

851ST **BMB SQDN**

•490th Bombardment Group (Heavy)•
•Station No.134•
Eye A/F-Suffolk
•Campaigns•
Air Offensive-Europe • Normandy
Northern France • Rhineland
Ardennes-Alsace • Central Europe
•Assigned Eighth AF•
April, 1944-June, 1945

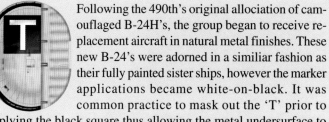

Following the 490th's original allociation of camouflaged B-24H's, the group began to receive replacement aircraft in natural metal finishes. These new B-24's were adorned in a similiar fashion as their fully painted sister ships, however the marker applications became white-on-black. It was common practice to mask out the 'T' prior to applying the black square thus allowing the metal undersurface to show through as the letter form once the mask had been removed.

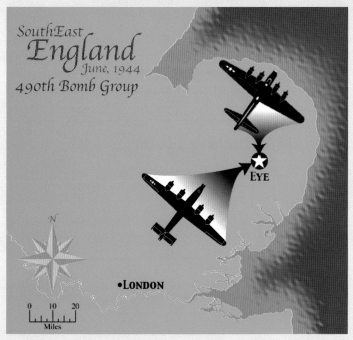

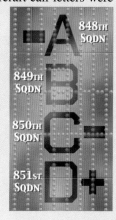

With the introduction of the 93rd Combat Bomb Wings high-visibility color tactical markings, the 490ths' B-24's were 'redecorated' to conform to the new unit identification system. As with their B-17 counterparts, the top one-third of each tail section received a coat of red paint. On camouflaged ships the bottom two-thirds were painted an overall white, while natural metal finishes received no paint in this area. Individual aircraft call-letters were now applied with black paint and measured approximately 24" in height. The use of additional squadron identifying symbols were adopted during this same time period. The 'plus' symbol employed by the 851st Bomb Squadron varied considerably in both weight and size but nevertheless remained unmistakable as to its' origin. The 'bars' adopted by the 848th and 850th squadrons were a different matter altogether. These symbols more closely resembled a large black brick than an accustomed bar/minus image. If nothing else, they were different.

The 490th Bomb Group was yet another of those units within the structure of the Eighth Air Force that avoided the use of SD110 squadron codes. Being relatively late arrivals to the European Theater of Operations may have had a great deal to do with this factor. By the summer of 1944, virtually all units comprising the Eighth had adopted their own distinctive group marking system, and thus individual aircraft identification within each unit may have become a discretionary issue. Whatever the reason, the bombers of 490th did not adopt a 'traditional' squadron code system until after Germany's surrender on the eighth of May, 1945. As stated on the previous page, with the exception of a call-letter, the 490th did not employ any means of individual aircraft identification whatsoever during the period following their initial deployment in England. With the groups new high-visibility color tactical marking pattern however, the 490th did adopt a plus/minus (bar) code mechanism designed to assist in air-to-air and ground control aircraft identification.

The two photographs to the immediate left provide good glimpses at both the first and second pattern applications of the 490th Bomb Groups tactical markings. Note that the 'plus' symbol on the tail of this particular B-17 measures in at about the same height as the call-letter itself. In the lower photo the call-letter appears to be approximately 24" in height. Early applications of this symbol within the 490th seemed to have run the gambit size-wise, ranging anywhere from as small as 12" to that of a more standard size such as depicted in this war time photograph.

491 ꜱᴛ BOMBARDMENT GROUP (HEAVY)

High-visibility tail markings were adopted by the 491st upon the groups arrival in England. The white stripe measured 36" in height with call-letters averaging in at around 24". The Circle 'Z' wing devise had a diameter of 78" and incorporated a 48" tall letter. On camouflaged applications this letter could be either Insignia Blue or black, however the majority of aircraft assigned to the 491st consisted of natural metal finishes. The SD110 squadron codes were 48" tall and applied in a light-grey paint on camouflaged ships and with black on metal surfaces.

The tail surfaces of 491st B-24's alternated between Medium Green (No.42) and a somewhat darker shade used by the R.A.F. plus a 'home brewed' concoction that was apparently the result of mixing an appropriate amount of available colors. This mixture proved somewhat less than satisfactory for the most part, as the so-called 'grass-green' had a decidedly sickly pallor about it.

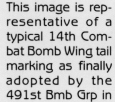

This image is representative of a typical 14th Combat Bomb Wing tail marking as finally adopted by the 491st Bmb Grp in the last few months of the European conflict. This pattern had formerly been displayed on 492nd Bomb Group aircraft prior to that units being broken up with the headquarters structure subsequently reassigned to the special covert operations unit designated Operation Carpetbagger.

| 852ᴺᴰ BMB SQDN | 853ᴿᴰ BMB SQDN | 854ᵀᴴ BMB SQDN | 855ᵀᴴ BMB SQDN |

•491ST BOMBARDMENT GROUP (HEAVY)•
'THE RINGMASTERS'
•STATION NO.366
METFIELD A/F-SUFFOLK
•STATION NO.143•
NORTH PICKENHAM A/F-NORFOLK
•CAMPAIGNS•
AIR OFFENSIVE-EUROPE • NORMANDY
NORTHERN FRANCE • RHINELAND
ARDENNES-ALSACE • CENTRAL EUROPE
•ASSIGNED EIGHTH AF•
JANUARY, 1944-JUNE, 1945

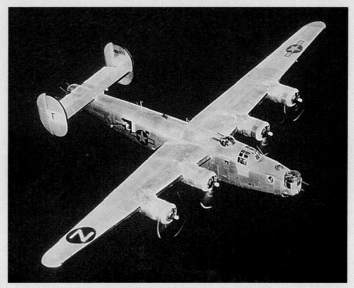

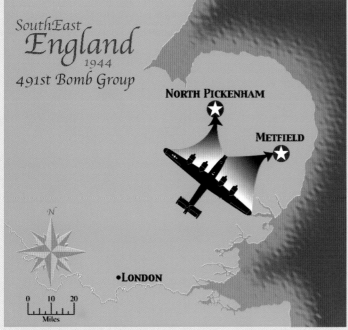

This aerial shot affords a good look at the relative size and placement of the 490ths' original Circle 'Z' wing marker. Some of the letters contained within these devices were applied with rounded edges, others were of a sharp edge variety. Refer to the wing illustrations on the preceding page for a comparison of the two types.

Although the use of color as a means of squadron identification was never officially adopted by the 491st Bomb Group, two of its' squadrons did opt to employ painted cowling rings within their respective structures by the end of 1944. These applications were somewhat sporadic and were not inclusive of all aircraft within the squadrons. Although 490th headquarters had apparently given provisional permission to employ the use of color in this manner, the 853rd and 855th Squadrons apparently made a decision not to participate in this program.

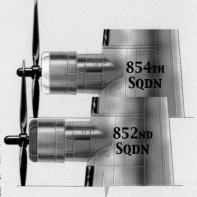

It took the 491st Bomb Group a little while to settle in after reaching Great Britain. They were first billeted at North Pickenham Air Field, but this lasted less than six weeks. They next moved to Metfield, where their stay lasted only four months, from 15 April thru 15 August. The group finally came to roost right back where they had started from, North Pickenham, and here they would remain until the wars end. The 491st originally began their combat operations with the 95th Combat Bombardment Wing, but this unit was deactivated in August of 1944. The 95th CBW had been activated in England on the 12th of December 1943 and had only been operational for approximately six weeks prior to being shut down. The 489th and 490th Bomb Groups were the only two combat units actually assigned to the 95th CBW, which was subsequently disbanded on 28 August, 1945.

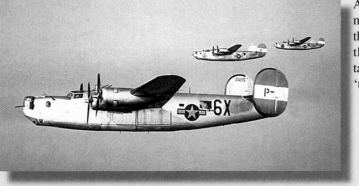

An up-close look at the tactical markings of a B-24H belonging to the 854th Bomb Squadron. Note that the 'bar' in this particular tail call-letter application is of a 'trailing' mode. (see chart below)

The 490th BG was officially placed under the command of the 14th Combat Bombardment Wing immediately after the 95th CBW ceased its own combat operations. The group was to remain a permanent component of the 95th throughout the remainder of the war. The 490th continued however to display its' original green tail and horizontal white stripe tail configuration until March, 1945. At that time it adopted color markings consistent with the 14th CBW.

The visual to the right represents the squadron identification plus/minus (bar) symbols utilized by the 491st Bomb Group, and incorporated in conjunction with tail call-letters. In the case of the 853rd and 854th Squadrons, both methods of applying the 'bar' symbols were used concurrently.

	852ND SQDN
A	852ND SQDN
-B B	853RD SQDN
C- C̄	854TH SQDN
D+	855TH SQDN

14TH COMBAT BOMBARDMENT WING (H)

2ND BOMBARDMENT (AIR) DIVISION

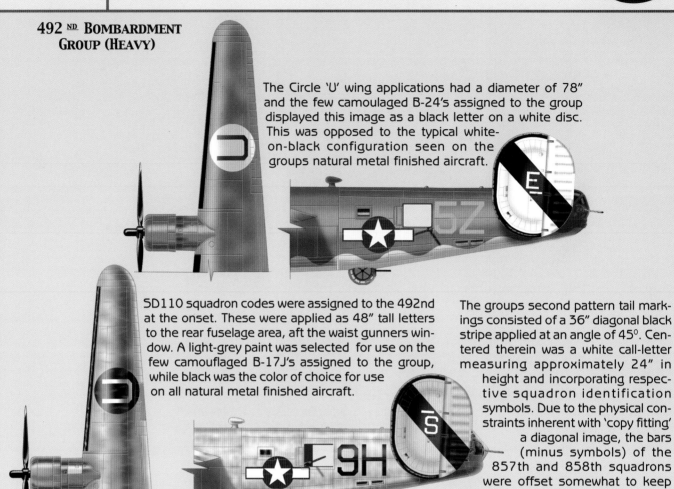

492 ND BOMBARDMENT GROUP (HEAVY)

The Circle 'U' wing applications had a diameter of 78" and the few camoulaged B-24's assigned to the group displayed this image as a black letter on a white disc. This was opposed to the typical white-on-black configuration seen on the groups natural metal finished aircraft.

SD110 squadron codes were assigned to the 492nd at the onset. These were applied as 48" tall letters to the rear fuselage area, aft the waist gunners window. A light-grey paint was selected for use on the few camouflaged B-17J's assigned to the group, while black was the color of choice for use on all natural metal finished aircraft.

The groups second pattern tail markings consisted of a 36" diagonal black stripe applied at an angle of 45°. Centered therein was a white call-letter measuring approximately 24" in height and incorporating respective squadron identification symbols. Due to the physical constraints inherent with 'copy fitting' a diagonal image, the bars (minus symbols) of the 857th and 858th squadrons were offset somewhat to keep from reducing their overall length.

| 856TH BMB SQDN | 857TH BMB SQDN | 858TH BMB SQDN | 859TH BMB SQDN |

•492ND BOMBARDMENT GROUP (HEAVY)•
'THE CARPETBAGGERS'
•STATION NO.143•
NORTH PICKENHAM A/F- NORFOLK
•STATION NO. 179•
HARRINGTON A/F-NORTHHAMPTONSHIRE
•CAMPAIGNS•
AIR OFFENSIVE-EUROPE • NORMANDY
NORTHERN FRANCE • SOUTHERN FRANCE
RHINELAND • CENTRAL EUROPE
•ASSIGNED EIGHTH AF•
APRIL, 1944-JUNE, 1945

Most of the B-24's consigned to the 492nd featured natural metal finishes. However a handful of camouflaged B-24J's did reach the group and those that did displayed, for a very brief period, the Circle 'U' tail marker. This was a 69" disc with a 36" black letter.

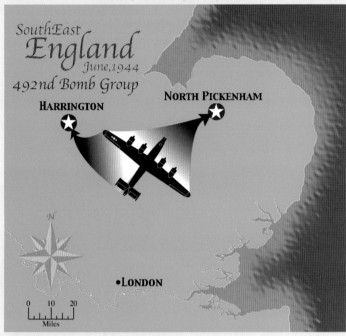

The graphics above depict the use of symbols adopted by the 492nd BG and incorporated with individual aircraft call-letters. These were in addition to the SD110 squadron codes which were prominently displayed on the rear fuselage area of all 492nd B-24's.

This is an interesting photo in that it poses several questions. The serial number on the outfacing port fin appears to have been repainted higher up on the tail than the original factory application. From this image it is unclear as to whether this occurred before or after the addition of the diagonal stripe.

As a conventional Eighth Air Force bombardment unit the 492nd Bomb Group had a very brief career. The 492nd entered combat on May 11, 1944 and were removed from combat the following August. During slightly less than four months of bombing operations the group got pretty well beat-up, losing fifty-seven of its' aircraft to direct combat or combat related operations. On August 11th 1944 the 492nd Bomb Group, for all intent and purpose, ceased to exist. The group was disbanded, its' equipment disbursed to other units, its' personnel transferred to other duty stations. On the surface it appeared as if the 492nd had faded into history. Looks however are often deceiving, especially in times of war. This is where the actual unit history of the group gets real cloudy. Select personnel from the 492nd were transferred to Harrington Air Field and subsequently reconstituted as a group on August 13th. The 'new' 492nd was actually comprised of elements of the former 801st Bomb Group (Provisional) which included the mysterious 36th and 406th Bomb Squadrons, both of which had recently experienced heavy combat losses themselves. This newly consolidated unit would continue the work begun by the 801st, preforming special missions in conjunction with both the American OSS (Office of Strategic Services) and the British SOE (Special Operations Executive). In other words, covert operations!

Due to the nature of these operations, normal tactical markings were removed from all 492nd aircraft, with the exception of the preexisting squadron codes which the group continued to display.

The tail section of the B-24 in the photo above still bears the remants of the original Circle 'U' group tactical marker. When the 492nd adopted the diagonally striped tail, many of the groups aircraft simply had this new pattern applied directly over the existing image.

493RD BOMBARDMENT GROUP (HEAVY)

Painted propeller bosses were employed by the 493rd BG at an early stage.

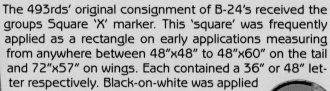

The 493rds' original consignment of B-24's received the groups Square 'X' marker. This 'square' was frequently applied as a rectangle on early applications measuring from anywhere between 48"x48" to 48"x60" on the tail and 72"x57" on wings. Each contained a 36" or 48" letter respectively. Black-on-white was applied to camouflaged aircraft, white-on-black to those ships with natural metal finishes.

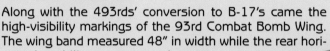

Along with the 493rds' conversion to B-17's came the high-visibility markings of the 93rd Combat Bomb Wing. The wing band measured 48" in width while the rear horizontal stabilizers measured 36". The tail band ascended from the fuselage approximately 36". A single 18" tall call-letter was applied in the top one-third of the tail section. In place of the normal SD110 squadron code on the fuselage there was a 48" tall black squadron 'call-sign'. The ships tail 'call-letter' preceded by the fuselage 'call-sign' served in place of the more traditional SD110 codes until these were finally adopted wars end.

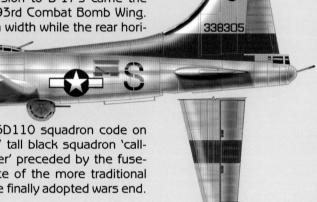

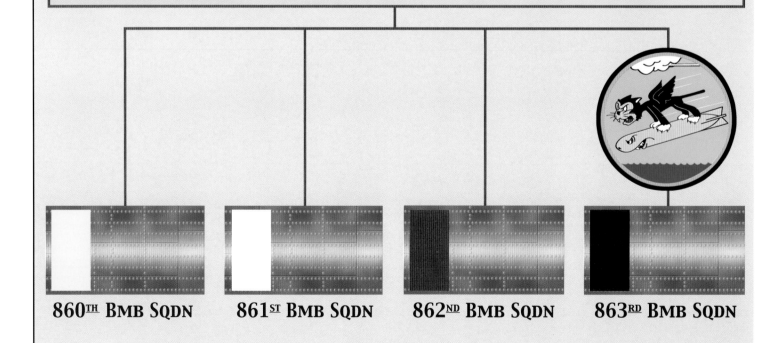

860TH BMB SQDN   **861ST BMB SQDN**   **862ND BMB SQDN**   **863RD BMB SQDN**

•493RD BOMBARDMENT GROUP (HEAVY)•
'HELTON'S HELLCATS'
•STATION NO.152•
DEBACH A/F-SUFFOLK
•CAMPAIGNS•
AIR OFFENSIVE-EUROPE • NORMANDY
NORTHERN FRANCE • RHINELAND
ARDENNES-ALSACE • CENTRAL EUROPE
•ASSIGNED EIGHTH AF•
JANUARY, 1944-JUNE, 1945

Three variations of patterns as would have been displayed on the tail fins of 493rd BG B-24's prior to the groups transition to B-17's.

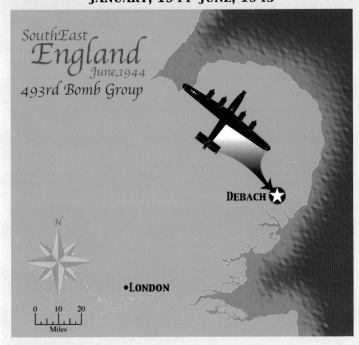

SouthEast
England
June, 1944
493rd Bomb Group

DEBACH

•LONDON

0 10 20
Miles

N

From the very beginning of their combat operations the 493rd Bomb Group employed the use of painted propeller bosses as an additional means of determining individual aircraft squadron assignment.

The 493rd Bomb Group holds two particularly unique distinctions within its' relatively brief history. This was the last bomb group to be placed on operational status within the structure of the Eighth Air Force. The other interesting footnote is that the 493rd flew their first combat operation on the Sixth of June, 1944, the day Allied ground forces stormed ashore on the beaches of Southern France. The 493rd originally trained and deployed to England with an inventory of 'H' and 'J' series B-24's. The group did in fact enter combat with this aircraft and continued to fly the Liberators until these were replaced with Flying Fortresses' in September of 1944.

This photograph gives a good look at the starboard side of a 493rd B-17. Note that the fuselage code designating the 861st Bomb Squadron is positioned just forward the waist gunners window. This is representative of a typical application of this particular marking devise within the 493rd Bomb Group on all their replacement B-17G's.

Although the 493rd did not adopt formal squadron codes until after the cessation of hostilities, they did incorporate within their unit a means of squadron identification in addition to the use of colored propeller bosses. Each squadron was assigned a letter and this symbol constituted a 'call-sign' which, when used in conjunction with the aircraft's tail letter, served to effectively identify individual aircraft. This method was employed with the groups B-17's only.

Note: The only squadron insignia for this group was originally designed for the 13th Antisubmarine Squadron (H) which was this units previous designation. It was reconstituted the 863rd Bomb Squadron (H) on 1Nov43 and assigned to the 493rd Bomb Group.

ACKNOWLEDGEMENTS:

Air Force Historical Research Agency, Maxwell AFB

2nd Air Division Memorial Library

8th Air Force Photo Archives

Maxwell AFB / Photo Archives

Museum of the Air Battle, Czech Republic

United States Air Force Museum / Photo Archives Div.

Wright-Patterson AFB / Military Museum

www.b24.net: Robert Books

USAAF Bomb Group Associations;

91st Bomb Group: Ray Wood•John A. Feairheller• Paul Chryst

92nd Bomb Group: Alfons Eignmann

94th Bomb Group: Byron Trent

95th Bomb Group:

100th Bomb Group: Jim Marsteller

303rd Bomb Group Association

323rd Bomb Group: Colne Valley (Earls Colne Parish)

384th Bomb Group: Kenmore Rowe•Marc Poole•Jeanne Rinear

385th Bomb Group: Ed Stern•Bill Varnedoe

387th Bomb Group: Michael E. Smith•Kendall Thompson

392nd Bomb Group: T. Albino

398th Bomb Group: www.b17bomber.com

401st Bomb Group: SMSgt. Mark Brotherton•www.web-birds.com

445th Bomb Group Association

447th Bomb Group: John H. Kirkwood

448th Bomb Group: B.G. Patrica Everson

467th Bomb Group: Kevin Coolidge•Harold Weeks

490th Bomb Group: 'Moofy' in the UK

A special thanks to...

Lead Pilot: Lt. H.C. 'Pete' Henry
66th and 67th Bombardment Squadrons
44th Bombardment Group
Second Combat Bombardment Wing
Second Bombardment (Air) Division
U.S. Eighth Air Force
32 combat missions /April, 1944-May, 1945

BIBLIOGRAPHY:

Theo Boiten and Martin Bowman
 ' Battles with the Luftwaffe'

Martin Bowman
 'B-24 Liberator-1939-45'
 'Castles in the Air'
 'B-17 Flying Fortress Units of the Eighth Air Force',vol's 1&2

Mike Bailey with Tony North
 'Liberator Album / B-24's of the 2nd Air Division-USAAF'

Kit C. Carter / Robert Mueller
 'The Army Air Forces in World War II
 Combat Chronology- 1941-1945'

Pat Carty
 'Secret Squadrons of the Eighth'

Robert F. Dorr
 'B-24 Liberator Units of the Eighth Air Force'

Roger A. Freeman
 'The Mighty Eighth'
 'The Mighty Eighth in Color'

Hearst Publications / Robert Lash Robbins
 'War Insignia Stamp Album', vol 3

Gerard Hubbard
 'Aircraft Insignia, Spirit of Youth'
 National Geographic Magazine-June, 1943

Dr. M. Maurer
 'Air Force Combat Units of World War II'
 'Combat Squadrons of the Air Force / World War II'

Poststamp Publishing Co. / Robert Lash Robbins
 'Combat Insignia Stamps of the United States Army & Navy'
 'War Insignia Stamp Album', vol 2, & 4

Charles A. Ravenstein
 'The Organization and Lineage of the United States Air Force'

Robert Redding / Bill Yenne
 'Boeing- Planemaker to the World'

Jerry Scutts
 'B-26 Marauder Units of the Eighth and Ninth Air Forces'

Simon & Schuster Publishing
 ' Official Guide to the Army Air Forces'

Hans-Henri Stapfer
 'Strangers in a Strange Land'

Untied States Air Force
 'The United States Strategic Bombing Surveys-European War'

War Department / Air Corps Field Manual-FM 1-10

'The Angry Skies'
In Honor Of Those That Served

From our own farms, towns and cities they came
these were not mystic warriors of legends fame.
Together they banded one and all,
together in answer to freedoms call.
Their boyish dreams they set aside
to fight in distant angry sky's.

-R.A.Watkins '03-

* These organizational structures were originally constituted as 'Bombardment Divisions' Aug'43. They were not redesigned 'Air Divisions' until Dec '44.

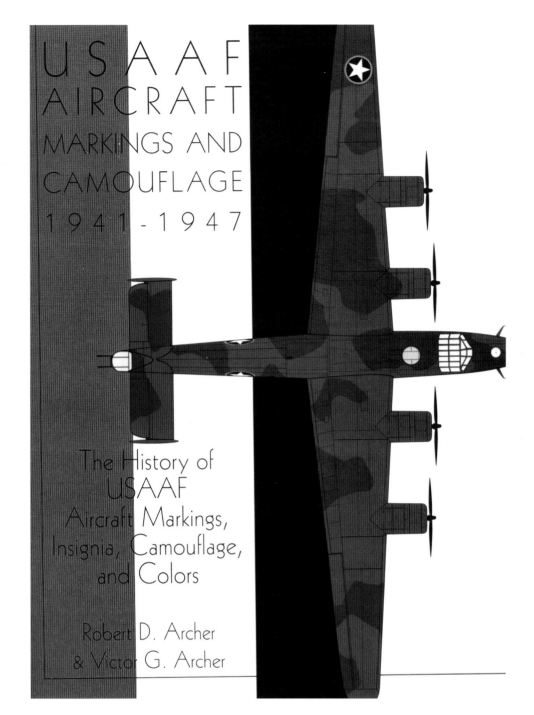

USAAF Aircraft Markings and Camouflage 1941-1947
The History of USAAF Aircraft Markings,
Insignia, Camouflage, and Colors
Robert D. Archer & Victor G. Archer

Covers the USAAF, pre-war and post-war, up to the fomation of the independent USAF in 1947.
All schemes are shown in full color, as three-view drawings where applicable. The numerous
official technical orders are given, presenting their complete progression for the first time. An
indispensable reference for historians, restorers of USAAF aircraft, museums, and modelers.
Size: 9" x 12" ■ over 480 color and b/w photos, 39 color illustrations ■ 352 pp.
ISBN: 0-7643-0246-9 ■ hard cover ■ $79.95